THE
NEW TESTAMENT
CHURCH

Fourth Edition

THE
NEW TESTAMENT
CHURCH

Fourth Edition

by

EVERETT FERGUSON

DESERT WILLOW PUBLISHING

The New Testament Church, Fourth Edition

By Everett Ferguson

Desert Willow Publishing,
P.O. Box 7719, Abilene, TX 79608, USA
http://www.desertwillowpublishingonline.com
desertwillowpublishing@gmail.com

Paperback ISBN: 978-1-939838-29-2

E-book ISBN: 978-1-939838-30-8

Library of Congress Control Number: 2016955229

The photographs on the front and back covers were taken by Dr. Everett Ferguson. The photograph on the front cover depicts Christ and the apostles from the chapel of Saint Aquilino, church of San Lorenzo, Milan, Italy; it is dated at the end of the fourth century. The photograph on the back cover depicts the Mosaic of Christ and the apostles in the triumphal arch from the Euphrasian basilica, Porec, Croatia; it is dated in the sixth century.

Indexes are by Patty Doyle.

INTRODUCTION

Much that is familiar to students of the New Testament doctrine of the church will be found in these lessons. But there is also an emphasis given to some neglected insights and features. The aim is to call attention to the Christ-centered nature of the church and everything about it. The corporate (group) nature of life in Christ is stressed as against the individual approach.

It is suggested that the student read through each lesson for its main points and then come back to study carefully the Scripture references in relation to each point. It is important to look up each passage, for this is a Bible based study. The series of lessons will also be helpful in developing a method of Bible study, if the student will make diligent use of a good concordance and a reference Bible. A good, recent Bible dictionary will also be helpful. Through the comparative study of passages of Scripture the common associations of ideas will lead to further insights and new appreciations for the Biblical teachings.

CONTENTS

Lesson 1

THE OLD TESTAMENT EXPECTATION

*"The Lord's house shall be established on top of the mountains...
and all nations shall flow into it."*
(Isaiah 2:2)

THE MESSIANIC HOPE

MESSIAH IS A HEBREW WORD meaning "anointed." Specially chosen servants of God in Old Testament times were marked out for their task by pouring olive oil on their heads. We read of anointing in the appointment of kings (1 Sam. 10:1; 16:1, 13) and in the consecration of priests (Ex. 29:7; 30:22–33). Prophets are also spoken of as anointed (Ps. 105:15), but apparently theirs was not a literal anointing with oil, rather a metaphorical one with the Holy Spirit (Isa. 61:1). The pouring out of oil was a sign of blessing, and this act marked out one for God's blessing and designated the person as the Lord's favorite. The meaning that this act had for the Hebrew people is indicated in Psalms 133:1–2 about the high priesthood.

When this Hebrew idea was expressed in Greek, the word used was *Christos* ("Christ"—John 1:41). Luke, writing for Gentile readers, who would be unfamiliar with the significance which the term had for the Jewish people, incidentally defined the meaning of "Christ" in Luke 23:35 where he speaks of "the Christ of God, his Chosen One."

In the Old Testament there is the hope that in the future there would be a time of blessing and a Redeemer of the people who would bring about these blessings. The One described is variously presented: Servant of the Lord (Isa. 53); Son of Man (Dan. 7:13–14.); the Branch of David (Isa. 11:1–2, 10).

Although the term "anointed" could be used of anyone chosen by God for his purposes (e.g. the Persian king Cyrus—Isa. 45:1), it was not used in the Old Testament specifically of the expected Redeemer. Since it was preeminently kings and priests who were the anointed leaders (Zech. 4:14), it was natural that as hopes came to be concentrated on an idealized king and priest that the term should be employed for this personage.

In the intertestamental literature there was a development of ideas found in the Old Testament. Some of these writings speak of a royal Messiah, a Davidic king, who would bring deliverance to the Jews (*Psalms of Solomon* 17–18). This seems to have been the most prevalent form of the messianic hope in Jesus' day. Other writings speak only of God himself intervening on behalf of his people with no specific mention of an agent through which his will is accomplished (*Jubilees* 1:19–28). Other documents present a supernatural figure arising at the end of the ages to execute God's purposes (*1 Enoch* 39–71; cf. Dan. 7). Among the members of the Qumran community (now known to us from the Dead Sea Scrolls) there appears to have been the expectation of two Messiahs—a son of David to exercise kingly rule, and a son of Aaron to give priestly leadership (*Rule of the Community* 9.11). With these two there may have been linked the thought of a prophetic forerunner.

The Christian sees Jesus as a fulfillment of all these pictures of the Messiah. He is son of David, God manifest in the flesh, the supernatural or heavenly man, and the ideal prophet, priest, and king.

THE MESSIANIC AGE

For the Jews what was important was the condition to be realized in the Messianic Age, of which the "Messiah" was only a part. For Christians it was the Person who "brings" the Age. The Age was realized in the Person of Jesus.

Part of the eschatological ("last events") hope of the Old Testament found expression in the conviction that God would make a *new covenant* with his people. The Israelites had broken the covenant God made with their fathers (Jer. 11:10; cf. 22:9), but God would make an "everlasting covenant with them" (Jer. 32:40; cf. Ezek. 16:60). This "everlasting covenant" is mentioned in passages which also speak of a special chosen leader: Isaiah 55:3, 4 (cf. Acts 13:34) and Isaiah 61:1–9 (Lk. 4:18–19). This new covenant would not be like the covenant made on the basis of the deliverance from Egypt at Sinai (Jer. 31:32) but would be a spiritual covenant (Jer. 31:33) involving a chosen relationship of knowledge (Jer. 31:34).

It would be a covenant of forgiveness in a way the old covenant was not (Jer. 31:34). This was another characteristic of the Messianic Age. It would be an age of forgiveness of sins. Ezekiel draws on the Old Testament ceremonial cleansing in order to describe the time when God will make his people clean and enable them to keep his ordinances (36:22–31). It would be a mistake to see in this passage which speaks in terms of Old Testament ritual practices the specific mode of a Christian's cleansing ("sprinkling," Ezek. 36:25; see Lesson 5), but it would also be a mistake not to see in this passage a clear reference to the future age of God's people. God will cleanse his people of all their filthiness. God's act of forgiveness was to be coupled with the people's repentance (Ezek. 36:31–32.).

One notices in Ezekiel an association of water with cleansing and of a new heart with the Holy Spirit. The association of the forgiveness of sins and the presence of the Holy Spirit is frequent in the Bible. The Messianic Age was also to be an age of the *Holy Spirit*.

Just as in Ezekiel, the cleansing must precede the reception of the Holy Spirit. Since God's Spirit is *holy*, he does not dwell where there is sin. The forgiveness of sins must precede the indwelling of the Holy Spirit. Isaiah 59:20–21 speaks of the coming of a Redeemer to Zion and the Lord making a covenant with his people: and that covenant will be the placing of the Lord's Spirit upon the people. It is interesting to note the use Paul makes of this passage in Romans 11:26–27. He cites the passage with the difference that he says that the covenant will be a "taking away of their sins." Some see Paul combining his quotation of Isaiah 59 with the new covenant passage of Jeremiah 31. Just possibly Paul is giving an interpretative quotation, seeing the significance of the bestowing of the Holy Spirit in the removal of sins. At any rate nothing could more clearly show the intimate association of forgiveness and the gift of the Holy Spirit for Paul than this usage of Old Testament prophecy.

Indeed the distinctive feature of the Messianic Age was to be the possession of the Holy Spirit (Joel 2:28–32, quoted by Peter in Acts 2:16–21). The Messiah himself was to be specially equipped with God's Spirit (Isaiah 61:1–2). Thus he could dispense forgiveness of sins and the Spirit to others.

THE MESSIANIC PEOPLE

There was no Messiah apart from a people. Of course, the characteristics of the Age to come implied a community. A covenant is made with a people; forgiveness of sins is granted to a people; and the Spirit rests upon a people. In the very nature of the Messianic Age there was implied a distinctive people of God. Thus in the very nature of Jesus as Messiah there is implied the conception of a church.

Old Testament words indicating community—*assembly, congregation, house*—occur frequently in contexts of the future hope. A feature of the expectation concerning the future time was the gathering of God's people which had been dispersed and an assembly of the nations. For particularly striking passages one may read Isaiah 43:1, 2, 5–9, 25; 56:8; and 60:4. The Greek translation of these verses employs the words which will be found in the New Testament in reference to the gathering and assembling of the Lord's people (Heb. 10:25; 2 Thess. 2:1).

There was not only to be a gathering of the righteous. There must also be a proclamation to the peoples (Isa. 52:7); God's people were to be a light to the nations (Isa. 49:6b); and there must be a bearing witness of God (Isa. 43:10).

CONCLUSION

Many Old Testament themes about the Age to Come find classic expression in the prophetic declaration which appears in two similar forms in Isaiah 2:2–4 and Micah 4:1–3.

The New Testament begins the story of the gospel with the ministry of John the Baptist (Mk. 1:1–8) in which there is a heightening of the Old Testament expectation (Matt. 3:1–12; Lk.1:5–79; John 1:19–34).

Jesus appeared as the Messiah (Mk. 8:29) and was anointed by the Spirit (Acts 10:38; Matt. 3:16–17; Lk. 4:18–21). He brought a new covenant (Matt. 26:28), forgiveness of sins (Mk. 2:5–11), and the Holy Spirit (John 1:33).

The new covenant brought by Jesus Christ meant an end to the Mosaic system of religion and the inauguration of a new age. It also meant the beginning of a new people under a new Lawgiver (Matt. 17:1–6; Gal. 3:22–25; Heb. 8:1–13; 2 Cor. 3:1–18).

REVIEW QUESTIONS

1. What is the meaning of the word Messiah? What is its Greek equivalent?

2. What individuals received an anointing in the Old Testament?

3. What was the religious significance of an anointing with oil?

4. Trace the development of the "messianic hope" in Judaism before New Testament times.

5. How does Jesus fulfill the expectations of the Old Testament about a "messianic" personage?

6. Name three principal characteristics of the Messianic Age in the Old Testament anticipation.

7. With the use of a concordance or reference Bible locate some passages where there is an association of the forgiveness of sins and the presence of the Holy Spirit.

8. Can you find other passages where the characteristics of the Messianic Age are found in association?

9. How does the presence of the Messiah demand the presence of a people also?

10. What was to be the task of the gathered people of God?

11. What implication does a "new covenant" have for the authority of the "old covenant" (of Moses)?

Lesson 2

THE ESTABLISHMENT OF THE CHURCH

"I will build my Church."
(Matthew 16:18)

JESUS' PROMISE

DURING JESUS' PERSONAL MINISTRY HE laid the groundwork for the church and prepared the nucleus of a community. As an authoritative teacher he gave a new law (Matt. 5–7) and declared by word and deed his personal significance for the kingdom of God (Matt. 12:28; 16:28; 10:32–33). By faith men became attached to him. He gathered his disciples and called twelve (Mk. 3:14) to be the basis of a new Israel (Matt. 19:28), even as old Israel had grown from the twelve patriarchs (Gen. 35:9–26).

Such activities by Jesus provoked discussion as to his identity (Matt. 11:2–3; John 10:24). It was in such a context of discussion about Jesus' identity that Peter made his confession that Jesus was the Messiah (Matt. 16:13–16). Then Jesus made the promise, "Upon this rock I will build my church" (Matt. 16:18). The messiahship of Jesus is the foundation of the church.

As Jesus makes clear in a number of passages, messiahship meant for him, contrary to what it meant for many Jews of his time, that he must die and be raised. Observe that it was immediately after the disciples' confession that Jesus was indeed the long sought Christ that he began to teach them what this meant—namely, that he "must go to Jerusalem and suffer many things from the elders and chief priests and scribes, and be killed, and on the third day be raised" (Matt. 16:21). Consider further Luke 24:45–46. Before the messianic people could be called into a separate existence Jesus had to fulfill this work of the Messiah.

It was the death of Jesus as the suffering Servant-Messiah (Isa. 53) that made him the foundation of the church. Several New Testament passages reflect responses to Jesus' death by their use of "stone" or "rock" quotations from the Old Testament. A "crucified Christ" was a "stumbling block to Jews" (1 Cor. 1:23). But this was according to prophecy. Peter brings together a string of quotations in 1 Peter 2:4–8. Jesus is that "living stone, rejected by men but in God's sight chosen and precious" (designations of the Messiah). He is the "cornerstone chosen and precious" (Isa. 28:16). He was the "stone which the builders rejected" whom "God has made the head of the corner" (Ps. 118:22; Mk. 12:10–11). For those who do not believe, he is "a rock that will make them fall" (Isa. 8:14). Paul uses the last passage in Romans 9:32–33. Jesus' death (the work of the Messiah) made him the rock that was the foundation of the church. It was a stone of stumbling, rejected by the Jewish rulers, but God made that stone the head of the corner. Jesus was the essential climax of God's purposes. He is the one to whom the other "living stones" (1 Pet. 2:5) are joined and from whom they take their origin. Thus "other foundation can no man lay than that which is laid, which is Jesus Christ" (1 Cor. 3:11; cf. Eph. 2:20–22).

THE FULFILLMENT AT PENTECOST

It is instructive to go from the Old Testament expectation and the promise of Jesus to Acts 2 and observe the sense of fulfillment. There we find the first public proclamation of Jesus as the Christ (Acts 2:36). Jesus had explained the necessity for his death (Lk. 24:45–46) and announced that his disciples were "witnesses" (Lk. 24:48). One should keep in mind that Luke and Acts were originally two volumes of one work. When one reads continuously from the last chapter of Luke through the first two chapters of Acts the continuity of the same themes emerges. Thus

Jesus in Acts 1:8 further announces that the disciples were to be his "witnesses…to the end of the earth." This was to be the task of the new Israel (Isa. 49:6; Acts 13:47; 26:23). And so the disciples gave their witness (Acts 2:32). After Peter proclaimed the death and resurrection in his sermon, he announced, "God has made him both Lord and Christ, this Jesus whom you crucified" (Acts 2:36). Before this time people had confessed faith in Jesus, but Jesus had not allowed them to proclaim this fact (Matt. 16:20). Perhaps the reason Jesus did not want this proclaimed as yet was that he had not yet performed the work which he came to do in dying for people. At any rate, it is only after his death that God "took the wraps off" and commissioned Jesus' disciples to preach in his name, and only in Acts 2 is the declaration of the messiahship made for all to hear.

The messiahship was demonstrated in the resurrection. He was "designated Son of God in power…by his resurrection from the dead" (Rom. 1:4). The Christ had to "suffer and on the third day rise from the dead" (Lk. 24:46). The burden of Peter's message in Acts 2 is to prove Jesus' resurrection and so demonstrate his messiahship. "You crucified" him, "but God raised him up" (Acts 2:23–24). Jesus was "attested to you by God with mighty works" (Acts 2:22) which were signs of his being "God's chosen." Although rejected by men, God raised him in accordance with prophecy (Acts 2:25–31). The apostles were witnesses of that (Acts 2:32). It was by the resurrection that Jesus was made to be "the head over all things for the church" (Eph. 1:19–23). It is the resurrected Jesus that can declare, "All authority…has been given to me" (Matt. 28:18). Before the resurrection Jesus was not the head of the church. We may note that "head" in Hebrew denotes not just authority but also "origin, source." Jesus as the "firstborn from the dead" is the "head of the church" (Col. 1:18; Rev. 1:5), that is those who will be resurrected along with him (1 Cor. 15:23; Rom. 8:29) and who are thus called the "church of the firstborn ones who are enrolled in heaven" (Heb. 12:23).

The resurrected Christ gave a commission to his followers. Before this they had no mission in the world. They were now to "preach the gospel" (Mk. 16:15), and be "witnesses" (Lk. 24:48), and "make disciples" (Matt. 28:19). Thus they would gather a people. Indeed the gospel had been preached in promise to Abraham (Gal. 3:8), and Jesus had proclaimed the "gospel of God" (Mk. 1:14) in preparation. But the central facts of the gospel—the death, burial, and resurrection of Christ, as Paul outlines them (1 Cor. 15:1–5)—could only be proclaimed as accomplished events for the first time in Acts 2. Only then did the apostles have a gospel to preach. As they made disciples, Jesus would continue to create a community.

The "good news" of the gospel consists in the fact that by virtue of Christ's death and resurrection "whoever calls on the name of the Lord shall be saved" (Acts 2:21). The messianic people were to be a forgiven people. The death of Jesus brought forgiveness of sins (Eph. 1:7). The church is a "purchased people" (Acts 20:28). Acts 2 marks the beginning of the offer of forgiveness of sins in Jesus' name. Jesus had bestowed the Spirit in order to qualify the apostles to offer forgiveness (John 20:22–23). "Repentance and forgiveness of sins" was to be preached "in his name to all nations, beginning from Jerusalem" (Lk. 24:47). This was the offer which Peter made in Acts 2:38, where once more we find "repentance," "forgiveness of sins," and "the name of Jesus." Jesus had offered forgiveness directly while he was on earth (Mk. 2:1–12), and he confirmed that power by his miraculous signs. But people do not stand in the same relation to Jesus now. We, like the 3,000 in Acts 2, hear the words of forgiveness through the apostles. But the promise (Acts 2:39) is no less sure, for it is made "in his name." The church thus took its rise from the death of Jesus, inasmuch as it is a forgiven people and that forgiveness came through his death. The Messianic Age (Joel 2:28–32) is realized through the announcement and acceptance of his Person (Acts 2:36).

This forgiveness constituted a new covenant. Jesus at the Last Supper declared of the cup, "This is my blood of the covenant, which is poured out for many for the forgiveness of sins" (Matt.

26:28). Thus did the hope of Jeremiah (31:31–34) find its fulfillment. The shedding of blood brought forgiveness of sins (Heb. 9:22); before the death, the covenant was not established (Heb. 9:16–17). With the acceptance of the forgiveness of sins through the death of Jesus by 3,000 people in Acts 2 (note vv. 38, 40, 41) there came into existence the community of the new covenant.

The Messianic Age, as was seen in the preceding lesson, was also to be an age of the Holy Spirit. Jesus had promised to his Apostles the Spirit in a special way to qualify them for their work (John 20:22–23); indeed they were to wait until the power of the Holy Spirit came upon them before they began preaching (Lk. 24:49; Acts 1:4). The apostles were "baptized in the Holy Spirit" (Acts 1:5; 2:1–4) at "the beginning" (Acts 11:15–18) of the new age. Jesus also promised that all who believed in him would receive the indwelling of the Holy Spirit (John 7:38–39). Before the Spirit came there could not be the church. The Spirit incorporates one in the church (1 Cor. 12:13). But the gifts of the Holy Spirit had to await the glorification of Jesus. In Acts 2 Peter begins his sermon with the Spirit (quoting Joel 2:28–32 as fulfilled in the events of the day, Acts 2:16–21), declares that it is the Christ glorified to the right hand of God who "has poured out this which you see and hear" (Acts 2:33), and ends with the Spirit promising him to all baptized into Jesus (Acts 2:38–39; cf 5:32). The Holy Spirit had come upon selected individuals in Old Testament times, but with Acts 2 begins the coming of the Spirit upon all of God's people and his permanent indwelling among them (1 Cor. 3:16–17; 6:19; Eph. 2:22). Jesus as the Christ brings the Messianic Age—forgiveness of sins, a new covenant, and the gift of the Spirit.

Those who received Peter's message on the first Pentecost after the resurrection were baptized (Acts 2:40–41) and thus there came into existence in Jerusalem a new community, the people of the last days. The church was gathered (the manuscripts which read "church" in Acts 2:47 at least interpret correctly, even if this reading is not original). They began their corporate life together, coming together to hear the apostles teach and to share a common life, to pray and to break bread (Acts 2:42). Such was the beginning of Christian worship.

Those who date the beginning of the church to the ministry of John the Baptist or of Jesus confuse the preparations for the church with its actual existence and so date it too early. Those who date it to the gathering of the Gentiles (Acts 10–11) date it too late.

Today, wherever the messiahship of Jesus is preached in its fullness and that messiahship is confessed and expressed through baptism, the church is built in that place.

REVIEW QUESTIONS

1. What was the work of the Messiah as announced by Jesus?

2. Describe the dual aspect of Jesus as a rock—stumbling stone and cornerstone.

3. What justification is there for reading continuously from the end of Luke to the beginning of Acts? What is the advantage of doing so?

4. Why was the resurrection essential for the beginning of the church?

5. What commission did Jesus lay upon his followers? What are its basic contents?

6. What three characteristics of the Messianic Age found in the preceding lesson are true of the church? When did each of these characteristics become available to people generally?

7. What event did Peter single out in Acts 11:15 as marking "the beginning"?

8. How does this lesson already show the centrality of Christ for the understanding of the church?

9. When did Christian worship begin?

10. When and where is the church established today?

Lesson 3

CHRIST AND CHRISTIANS

"The disciples were called Christians."
(Acts 11:26)

OLD TESTAMENT TERMINOLOGY

THE NATURE OF THE CHURCH is rooted in Old Testament ideas about the people of God. The New Testament's continuity with and break with the Old Testament are both indicated by the way the Old Testament language is used in reference to Christians. The New Testament uses the same words used for God's people in the Old Testament but claims them for Christians. Christians are the "Israel of God" (Gal. 6:16).

The language of Exodus 19:5–6, when the covenant agreement at Sinai was made between God and Israel, is used in 1 Peter 2:9 in reference to the church—Christians are a "royal priesthood," "a holy nation," "God's own people." God's people, therefore, continue with the Christians. The true fulfillment of Old Testament teaching is found in the spiritual Israel: what was formerly said about God's people is said now about the church. "Not all who are descended from Israel belong to Israel, and not all are children of Abraham because they are his descendants" (Rom. 9:6–7). "We are the true circumcision, who worship God in spirit" (Phil. 3:3). "He is a Jew who is one inwardly, and real circumcision is a matter of the heart, spiritual and not literal" (Rom. 2:29).

This self-conscious claim to succeed old Israel is evident in other word usages. Christians are "the righteous remnant" about which Isaiah wrote. So Paul in Romans 9:27–29 quotes Isaiah 10:22–23 and 1:9 about the remnant that shall be saved. Christians are also the people of the new covenant prophesied by Jeremiah (31:31–34) as may be seen by Paul's language about a "new covenant" in 2 Corinthians 3:6–18 and the quotation of Jeremiah in Hebrews 8:6–13. Christians are also the "saints of the Most High" mentioned by Daniel (7:22) who possess "the kingdom" (Rev. 1:6, 9; Rom. 14:17).

THE NAME CHRISTIAN

As previously studied, the church comes in fulfillment of the Old Testament expectation about the "last days." The Messiah (Christ) is not separate from his people. Jesus pointed to the closeness of the relationship between himself and his people in Matthew 25:31–46, where he claims what is done for his brethren is done for him and vice versa.

This truth is very vividly seen in those messianic titles which are also the names of his people. There are many terms related to the Messiah which are also used of his people.

Thus, for example, Christians wear the name of Christ. The term "Christian" means "of, or belonging to, Christ." It is formed from "Christ" and a Latin suffix *ianus* which, under the Roman Empire, was frequently borrowed in Greek. This suffix indicates that one belonged to the person to whose name the ending was added. It thus served as a special substitute for the possessive genitive; the better Greek phrase "those of Christ" is more common—1 Corinthians 1:12; 15:23; Galatians 5:24. This kind of word formation was in general use; one of the instructive parallels is *Caesarianus*, literally one who belonged to Caesar, a designation for an imperial slave. These "Caesarians" often had important administrative posts under the Empire. Thus Christians are the servants of the Messiah; theirs is a royal title. The name "Christian" was first used in Antioch (Acts 11:26), and that may be significant, for at Antioch the universalism of the new people of God composed of both Jews and Greeks was first realized.

The word "called" in Acts 11:26 was frequently used of divine revelations (as in Matt. 2:12) and may suggest a divine calling of his name on the Lord's people.

Jesus is the "Anointed One" (Christ), receiving an anointing of the Holy Spirit at his baptism (Matt. 3:16 and parallels). Thus equipped, Jesus carried out his messianic mission. Only with his resurrection had he performed the work of the Messiah, so that then God made him "both Lord and Christ" (Acts 2:36) and "declared him the son of God with power" (Rom. 1:4). Even so Christians who wear Christ's name "have an anointing from the Holy One" (1 John 2:20), like their Lord, not with oil, but with the Holy Spirit (2 Cor. 1:21–22). Early Christian writers did not hesitate to speak of Christians as "little Christs."

OTHER TITLES

Jesus as the Messiah is King (John 19:14; Lk. 19:38; Mk. 11:9–10; Rev. 19:16). His people therefore are in his kingdom (Col. 1:13). The basic idea of kingdom is not "realm," as we tend to think in English, but "reign." The "kingdom of God" proclaimed by Jesus in the Gospels refers to the kingly rule, or royal authority, of God. This kingly power of God exercised through Christ creates a people, the church. Thus those who are in Christ share in his kingdom (Rev. 1:4–9) and thus in his Messianic functions ("The saints shall judge the world," 1 Cor. 6:2; 2 Tim. 2:12).

Jesus is also high priest (Heb. 7:11–8:7; 9:11–14, 23–28; 10:11–14). His people therefore form a priesthood (Rev. 1:6; 1 Pet. 2:5, 9).

Kingdom and priesthood are collective concepts. Some of Jesus' individual messianic titles are also used of Christians. Jesus is "the Elect One," or "the Chosen One" (Lk. 23:35; 1 Pet. 2:4). Christians are "the elect ones," or the "chosen ones" (Col. 3:12; Rom. 8:33; Rev. 17:14). Jesus is "the Holy One" of God (Mk. 1:24; John 6:69; Acts 3:14). Christians are "the holy ones," or "saints" (Rom. 16:15; 2 Cor. 1:1; Eph. 5:3). Jesus is God's

"Beloved" (Matt. 3:17; Lk. 9:35; cf. Eph. 1:6). Christians are God's "beloved ones" (Rom. 1:7; Eph. 5:1).

The relationship between Christ and Christians may be illustrated further by the terms "Son" and "sons." Jesus is "the Son of God" (John 1:18), and Christians are also "sons" (Lk. 6:35; Rom. 8:14). He is the First-born One (Col. 1:15), and the church is made up of "firstborn ones" who are enrolled in heaven (Heb. 12:23). Galatians 3:26–27 makes it clear how people become sons. Baptism "into Christ" means that one has "put on Christ," he is "in Christ Jesus." If one is in Christ, he is "Christ's" so that the nature of Christ becomes his nature. Since Christ is Son, the Christian shares in his sonship.

The same principle may be applied to the other terms above. A concordance will reveal many other passages beyond those given as examples. But notice the consistent usage. The same word is used in the original language for both Christ and Christians, a fact sometimes obscured in the translations. But with few exceptions the singular is used exclusively for Christ, and the plural is used for his people. This word usage shows the difference between Christ and Christians—he is singularly and uniquely God's Son, Beloved, Saint, and Chosen one. A Christian as an individual does not possess this quality in relation to God. Yet the fact that the same word is used of them shows the association of the disciples with their Master. What is said of him is true of his people. They are sons, beloved, saints, chosen ones. But these things are not true of their own nature. They are true only through union with him, only "in Christ." The church derives its nature from Christ, but the church is not Christ. If the church tries to be its own authority it will forget this relationship.

The results of this study have importance for the nature of the church. It is what its Lord is. It is what it is because he is what he is. The nature of the church is derivative. The church is what it is only because of what Christ is. Christians are partakers of the nature of him whose they are. Furthermore, this is not an individualistic quality. They are saints and sons, beloved and elect, only collectively, not individually. Thus in the New

Testament Christians are referred to as "saints," but never is a single Christian called a "saint." Such quality is possessed only because he is a part of the church, the gathered people of God. All qualities shared with Christ are only "in him." One is a "saint," or any of these other titles, not because of anything he is or has done, but because he derives this quality from Christ. Of course, the task of the Christian life is to become fully what by the gift of Christ we are. The nature of Christians is the nature of Christ; but this is not possessed independently, it is only by incorporation in him.

"He who sanctifies and those who are sanctified have all one origin. This is why he is not ashamed to call them brethren" (Heb. 2:11).

It is a later and un-Biblical usage to individualize the word "saint" as a title referring to a special class of "super Christians." The Bible never speaks of "Saint Matthew," "Saint Paul," "Saint Elizabeth," or others. The use of "Saint" as a title belongs to Christ alone, "the Holy One" (John 6:69), and these individuals, as all Christians, are saints, "holy ones," by being united with him. The other titles of Christ and Christians have not been similarly abused, but the same principle applies to them.

The passage which perhaps brings out best the main thought of this lesson is Jesus' discussion built around the thought, "I am the vine and you are the branches," in John 15:1–11. In a spiritual paradox Jesus is the whole vine, just as he is the whole church, yet his people are branches of the vine. They receive their life from him and bear fruit in him; apart from him they are not of the vine. They have life, they are what they are only in union with Christ. Christ brings into existence extensions of himself. Where Christ is, there is the church.

Christ in an act of grace extends his qualities to his people so that they receive as a gift his status before God. The church derives its nature as well as its origin (Lesson 2) from Christ.

REVIEW QUESTIONS

1. How does the New Testament use of Old Testament terminology for the people of God show both a continuity and a discontinuity between the Old Testament and the New?

2. What are some of the Old Testament designations for the people of God used in the New Testament of the church?

3. What is the meaning of the word Christian? What is the word's origin? What does this word say about the nature of Jesus' disciples?

4. What is the evidence that "Christian" is a divinely given name? What other interpretations have been offered of Acts 11:26?

5. What does the word "kingdom" mean in Biblical usage (cf. Lesson 13)?

6. Are individual Christians ever termed priests in the New Testament?

7. What are some titles shared in common by Christ and his people? Check a concordance whether any of these is ever used in the singular of Christians.

8. How is it that one partakes of these qualities of Jesus?

9. What is the significance of these shared titles for the nature of the church? How is the church like and different from Christ?

10. How does the modern use of "Saint" as an individual title differ from Biblical usage?

11. What important teaching for the nature of the church and the relationship of Christ and Christians is contained in John 15:1–11?

Lesson 4

IMAGES OF THE CHURCH

"The churches of Christ"
(Romans 16:16)

THE WORD CHURCH

"CHURCH" (*ekklēsia*) IN CLASSICAL GREEK referred to the assembly of citizens in a Greek city state (cf. Acts 19:39). It was a political term with no particular religious associations. In actual usage the word did not carry the connotation of "called out." The separation of the church from the world is a correct theological idea taught in the New Testament (2 Cor. 6:17), but this feature of the church cannot be supported from the dictionary meaning of the word "church" itself. The basic meaning in New Testament times was simply "assembly," and in this meaning the word early appears in Christian literature for the actual assemblies of believers in Christ (1 Cor. 11:18; 14:19, 23, 34, 35). The great predominance of usage of the word in the New Testament is in its reference to the local church, whether assembled or not (e.g. Acts 11:22, 26; Gal. 1:22; Col. 4:16). The word had thus early become a technical term in Christian usage for the new people of God in a given locality. The new theological quality *ekklēsia* has in the New Testament comes from the Greek translation of the Old Testament, where it was used of the assembly of God's people Israel (Deut. 23:2–4, 9; Mic. 2:5; Ps. 89:5; cf. Acts 7:38). A corporate understanding was given the word from the Old Testament, in which the emphasis was on the solidarity of the group, rather than on the "collection of individuals." A Greek word was thus used, but its content was new and was supplied by the Jewish background where the assembly was the people of God (but it is doubtful that the word had acquired the connotation "people of God," for the emphasis seems to remain on the assembly or congregation even in the Old Testament passages). In the New Testament this corporate nature is present by virtue of the believers' relationship with Christ. In later books of the New Testament one finds the term "church" applied to the universal church (Eph. 1:22; Col. 1:24), even though its actual assembling must await the end time.

Since the word church by itself could refer to any assembly, frequently there is a descriptive or qualifying phrase added, identifying (but not properly "naming") the church as belonging to God or Christ (Rom. 16:16; 1 Cor. 1:2). Sometimes the reference is to the Christians who compose the church (1 Thess. 1:1; Heb. 12:23).

Lesson 3 looked at some of the terms applied to individual members of the church. The fellowship established with Christ and studied in Lesson 7 is described in the New Testament in various images. Several collective figures are applied to the Lord's people, such as the family of God (1 Tim. 3:15), the sheep and the sheepfold (John 10), the vineyard (Matt. 20–21). Three images are here selected for special examination.

BODY

One of Paul's favorite descriptions of the church was the body of Christ. In Romans 12:3–8 and 1 Corinthians 12:12–26 the emphasis is on the individual members of a body, each contributing its part to the functioning of the whole. In Ephesians 4:11–16 the emphasis is on the church as Christ's body, while Colossians 1:18 stresses that Christ is the head of the body, the church.

It may be argued that the "body of Christ" is more than a figure of speech, in that it describes a real relationship. It describes the basic character and nature of the church. The church consists of individuals who are in Christ because they have been baptized (1 Cor. 12:12–13; Rom. 12:4–5). The background of Paul's usage is probably to be found in the Hebrew idea of "corporate personality," in which a whole people may be viewed as one and in which one person may stand for and embody the whole (Gen. 10:6, 22; 36:1; Deut. 33; Jer. 31:15; Hos. 5:3; 11:1; Heb. 7:9; Rom. 9:13; cf. Lesson 3 on the messianic titles which are shared in common by Christ and Christians). The body finds its wholeness in Christ (as the branches and the vine in John 15). In the Old Testament concept of corporate personality the head stands for the whole. The head indicates the source ("beginning"—Ex. 12:2; Ezek. 16:25) and authority (first in rank—Ex. 6:14: Deut. 33:5). Christ is the principle of authority for the church because he is its creative source, and the church has its beginning and origin in him. Corollaries of his headship are the church's dependence on him and subordination to him.

Certain practical points are emphasized in the passages about the church as a body. Since Christ is head in "all things" (Eph. 1:22–23), he is the only indispensable part of the church. Indeed the whole is contained in him. Where he is, there is the church. There can be only one body, since there is only one Christ (Rom. 12:4, 5; 1 Cor. 12).

Each one in the church has a task to do (Eph. 4:16). There are different functions, a diversity contributing to unity (1 Cor. 12:28–31). Being united to the head, the body has no schism or discord, but rather sympathetic interest and mutual care (1 Cor. 12:24–26). Through the exercise of its gifts, the members of the body continue the ministry of Christ in the world. The church derives its life and being from him, and in so doing becomes his "body," the organ of his life in the world.

The importance of the church becomes obvious from this description. One cannot be subject to the head and united to Christ without being in his body. This body is the place of peace (Col. 3:15), reconciliation (Eph. 2:16), and salvation (Eph. 5:23).

35

The body of Christ concept has important implications for Christian ethics: since our bodies are joined to the Lord and belong to him, certain conduct is ruled out (Eph. 4:17–32; Col. 3:12–15; 1 Cor. 6:12–15). The idea of the body appears in important teaching in regard to baptism and the Lord's supper. It is also closely connected with another description of the church— the bride of Christ.

BRIDE

Although the church as the bride of Christ is referred to elsewhere (Rev. 21:2, 9), the fullest development of the idea is found in Ephesians 5:22–33.

The intimacy of the relationship of Christ and the church finds one of its closest human parallels in the intimacy of the marital union by which two become one flesh (Eph. 5:29–33). The love and authority of Christ, and the submission and response of the church are exemplified in the relationship. The headship is not an arbitrary authority but is an authority based on love. Only the greatest love can command the greatest obedience, but where the love is the greatest, the submission is freely rendered.

When Paul speaks of the "washing of water," and the adorning "without spot or wrinkle" (Eph. 5:26–27), he perhaps alludes to marriage customs in which the bride took a bath and put on new clothes before being presented to her husband. It is in keeping with the New Testament perspective which affirms both a "now" and a "not yet" that the bride is presented to Christ at baptism in Ephesians 5:26–27, but from another standpoint is not thought of as presented to him until the end time (Rev. 19:7, 8; Rev. 21:2). The "word" which accompanies the washing with water is probably the confession of faith (Heb. 10:22–23) rather than the baptismal formula or the preached word of the gospel. Such would fit the marriage imagery (with its exchange of vows) best.

BUILDING

The inadequacy of any single comparison in portraying all the facets of the nature of the church is seen in the way Paul speaks of building up the body (Eph. 4:16) and the author of Revelation describes the bride as a city (Rev. 21:9–27). The specific building to which New Testament authors compare the church is the temple (1 Cor. 3:9, 16–17; 2 Cor. 6:16; Eph. 2:19–22; 1 Pet. 2:5). Jesus designated his body a temple (John 2:19; cf. Mk. 14:58).

In the Old Testament God chose a place where his name was to be recorded and where his presence was particularly to dwell (Deut. 12:5–14; 1 Chron. 5:13–6:1; 6:41–7:3). The most holy place of the temple, where the *shekinah*, or glory of God's presence dwelt, was the mercy seat (Ex. 25:22; Ex. 40:34; Lev. 16:12–15), on which the atoning blood was offered annually. Jesus Christ is now God's glory among men (John 1:14; 2 Pet. 1:17), and he is the mercy seat (Rom. 3:25 is perhaps best to be understood as a reference to the mercy seat of the temple). The church of Christ is now the temple where God meets those who worship him.

The church, as the tabernacle and temple of the Old Covenant (Heb. 8:5), is built according to God's plan (1 Cor. 3:10–15). Christians are "living stones" (1 Pet. 2:5). Once more the inadequacy of metaphors is in evidence. It is obvious that this is not a real building, but a "spiritual house." The word church never refers to an actual building in the New Testament. Jesus Christ, to whom the other stones are joined, gives unity to the structure and is the cornerstone (1 Cor. 3:11; Eph. 2:20).

That God dwells there is what makes the church holy. The church is the dwelling place of God among people through the Holy Spirit (Eph. 2:22; 1 Cor. 3:16).

CONCLUSION

Not only are the same descriptive terms applied to Christ and Christians, but the church and Christ are brought into the most intimate possible union in Ephesians, especially in the descriptive terms studied in this lesson. These high privileges of the church are hers only "in Christ." The church does not have an independent importance, nor is it a relatively unimportant appendage to Christ. It has the utmost spiritual significance through union with Christ. In relation to Christ it is the body, bride, and building. As long as it is in subjection to him and in union with him, it is of supreme importance. But the church loses its importance when it does not submit to the authority of Christ and seeks to become its own authority. Thus all one does for Christ he does "in the church." And the church always sustains these relations to Christ not just when it is assembled. These images further show the importance of the individual Christian's relationship with others in the body. Christianity emphasizes individual responsibility, but it is not the radically individualistic religion some would make of it. One's personal relationship with Christ involves a corporate solidarity in the body.

These images of the church and others found in the New Testament continued in use in early Christian literature after the New Testament. Their usage demonstrate the continued importance of the church in early Christian thinking and the recognition of the relationship of the church to Christ.[1]

REVIEW QUESTIONS

1. Discuss the meaning of the Greek word *ekklēsia.*

2. Is there an emphasis on "called out" in the actual usage of the Greek word? How may this feature of the church properly be established?

---

1   Everett Ferguson, *Understandings of the Church* (Minneapolis: Fortress, 2016).

3. With the aid of a concordance consider the various uses of the word church in the New Testament.

4. Name some images of the church not discussed in this lesson.

5. From the Hebrew background, what is the emphasis in the idea of Christ as the head of the church?

6. What are some of the lessons taught by the description of the church as the body of Christ?

7. What are some of the lessons suggested by the metaphor of the bride applied to the church?

8. What is the Old Testament background to the description of the church as a temple?

9. What lessons about the nature of the church does the designation "temple" suggest?

10. What do all of these images have in common about the relationship of Christ and the church?

Lesson 5

BAPTISM

"By one Spirit were you all baptized into one body."
(1 Corinthians 12:13)

A S AN EXPRESSION OF FAITH and repentance one is baptized into Christ (Gal. 3:27; Acts 2:38). Baptism also places one in the church (1 Cor. 12:13). Baptism is particularly important for a study of the church, because it marks one's incorporation into the Messiah and into his people. It is also related to other aspects of the doctrine of the church. A full doctrine of salvation would require consideration of human sin, God's initiative in the atoning death of Christ, and the nature of human response to the gospel in faith and repentance. In the context of the study of the doctrine of the church, however, it is appropriate to give special attention to baptism.

THE GREAT COMMISSION

The Great Commission (Matt. 28:18–20; cf. Mk. 16:15–16; Lk. 24:47–48; John 20:22–23) was delivered in the midst of the great acts of God through Christ: death and resurrection, ascension and outpouring of the Holy Spirit. There was a divine plan of salvation which is worked out in Christ and his church (Eph. 1:3–14; 3:7–11). The great act of God's power for humankind was the raising of Christ from the dead (Acts 2:24–35; Eph 1:19–22) and so endowing him with all authority as messianic King (Matt. 28:18;

Rom. 1:4). This risen Lord gave the commission to make disciples and baptize (Matt. 28:19).

The content of the gospel was given by the risen Christ. The preaching was to be the message of his messiahship which will create the community (Lk. 24:46–47; 1 Cor. 15:1–8; see Lesson 2). That preaching remains God's power, God acting for human salvation (Rom. 1:16). Notice the emphasis in many New Testament passages on power in contexts about preaching (1 Cor. 1:18–24; 2:4–5; 2 Cor. 4:7; 13:3–4; Eph. 3:7; 1 Thess. 1:4–5). The word of the cross and resurrection is God's power, even as the resurrection itself was.

Preaching of this gospel calls people to God and Christ (2 Thess. 2:13–15; 1 Cor. 1:9), and so into the people of God. It does so when it is received in faith (Rom. 10:14–17; Heb. 4:2). The baptism commanded in the great commission (Matt. 28:19; Mk. 16:16) brings one into a special relationship with the Father, Son, and Holy Spirit. The establishment of the church is implicit in the command to baptize all nations. Baptism is part of the response to the preaching (Acts 8:35–36; 18:8; Col. 2:12). In baptism one is passive. It thus is still God's action and so God adds one to the church (Acts 2:41, 47; 5:14). At the beginning of the church on Pentecost, baptism was the response of faith to the preaching of Jesus as Messiah and the act which brought together the church.

Jesus' promise to be with his disciples "always" (Matt. 28:20) means that he still stands behind the message. His person continues to create a community based on a relationship of Lordship and discipleship. His presence means that his followers do not have authority on their own but continue in the relation of disciples to him (Matt. 23:8–12). Their task is to bring other people into a like relationship of discipleship with Jesus through baptizing and teaching.

DEATH, BURIAL AND RESURRECTION

A twofold scheme of the negative and positive benefits of baptism can be seen running through Romans 6–8 and Colossians

2–3. Baptism is a "putting to death" of the old person, a "putting off" of the old manner of life, a dying with Christ, a being buried with Christ. It is also a being "raised…to newness of life," a "putting on," a "being made alive" with him. We are united with Christ so that what happened to him historically happens to us spiritually and anticipates what will happen actually at his coming again. In baptism God does to a person what he did to Christ. The power of God which raised Christ is operative in baptism (Col. 2:12). One participates in that which forms the foundation of the church and by which Jesus accomplished the work of the Messiah (the death and resurrection), and so he is in-corporated into the messianic people.

The confession of faith in Jesus as "Lord" is a confession that God raised him from the dead (Rom. 10:9, 10). That confession is made not only with the lips but with the body as well. Baptism is an expression of faith in the working of God who raised Jesus from the dead (Col. 2:12; cf. further Eph. 1:19–20). That was the same kind of faith Abraham had (Rom. 4:17, cf. Heb. 11:19), and it is possession of the same quality of justifying faith that makes one a spiritual son of Abraham today (Rom. 4:20–25, Gal. 3:6–9), a part of the new Israel.

But baptism not only looks back to the founding act of the church. It also looks forward to Jesus' coming again when those who have been baptized will be raised (Rom. 8:11; 1 Cor 15:22–23; 1 Thess. 4:16). Baptism saves from the "wrath to come" (cf. Matt. 3:7). Those marked with this sign constitute the people of the age to come.

Paul reasons in Romans 6 that since we leave the sinful self in the water it is inconsistent to live any longer in sin. Thus baptism is a link between the once for all atonement of Jesus' death and the continuing life in Christ.

Anything other than immersion destroys this symbolism.

REMISSION OF SINS

The people of the new covenant are a forgiven people. This forgiveness is made possible by the blood (Matt. 26:28) of Jesus' sacrificial death. This forgiveness is made effective in the water (Acts 2:38; 22:16; Eph. 5:26; 1 Pet. 3:21). This is the negative benefit of baptism. Water was closely associated with cleansing in the Old Testament and was linked with the forgiveness of the new age by the prophets. Once more the outward act is a perfect symbol of the inner reality. As water cleanses the filth of the flesh, at the time of the outward cleansing God performs the work of the inner cleansing.

BESTOWAL OF THE HOLY SPIRIT

The Messianic Age was to be the Age of the Holy Spirit. The Spirit is one of the distinctive blessings of the Christian age and one of the promises which distinguished Christian baptism from John's baptism (Acts 19:2–3).

The gift of the Holy Spirit was promised to accompany water baptism (Acts 2:38; 5:32). The Spirit becomes the abiding possession of one converted (Gal. 4:6; 1 Cor. 6:19).

Even as blood and water are closely associated with cleansing, so water and the Spirit are closely associated in the Bible with the principle of life (see John 3:5; 7:38–39; Titus 3:5). It is the Spirit that gives life, and the Spirit does so in the water.

Here is the positive side of the benefits of baptism. The Holy Spirit imparts the energizing power of the new life in Christ (Rom. 8; Gal. 5:16–25). The Holy Spirit provides the connection between the "once for all" effects of baptism (pardon, justification, etc.) and their continuing relation to the Christian life. Thus growth in holiness is not solely a human achievement: one does not earn it and does not have to do it all alone. God helps, comforts, and strengthens his people. God gives not only gifts, but he gives himself.

There are no objective or psychological guarantees of the indwelling of the Spirit. The Christian knows this truth as he knows other things in the spiritual realm—through faith. He has the promise of God, and God cannot lie. Those who want or appeal to some other assurances in the form of inward feelings or external phenomena are betraying a lack of faith in the word and promise of God. It is the possession of the Spirit of Christ that makes the church the body of Christ.

INCORPORATION INTO THE CHURCH

According to 1 Corinthians 12:13 it is by the Spirit that we are baptized into one body. The Spirit makes us the body of Christ, the church. It is at this time that one is incorporated into the messianic community. The real administrator of baptism is the Holy Spirit. For that reason the human administrator is unimportant, as implied in 1 Corinthians 1:14–17. Paul does not depreciate the importance of baptism, only the importance of the human administrator.

Baptism places one in the Messiah. According to Galatians 3:26–27 it is because of faith that one is in the family of God. The time at which this faith results in one being placed in the family of God is stated to be baptism. One who has been baptized can know that he is a child of God because in baptism he "put on Christ," so he is "in Christ." Thus what is true of Christ becomes true of him, and what Christ is, he is. We are in his body because we are "in Christ."

Baptism is "in the name of Jesus Christ" (Acts 2:38). That is, it is done with reference to Jesus as the Messiah. It is an act of worship and obedience done with respect to Jesus. In baptism one confesses his faith in Jesus (Col. 2:12; Rom. 10:9–10). It is an act of repentance (Acts 2:38; see Mk. 1:4). The name of the Lord is pronounced over the one being baptized (Matt. 28:19; Acts 19:5–6). His name is given to one. This seems to be the force of Paul's statement in 1 Corinthians 1:13. One has the right to wear Christ's name (and no other) because he has been baptized in his name. He wears the name of "Christ" because he now belongs to him.

LATER DEVELOPMENTS

Writings from early Christian history after the New Testament describe baptism as an immersion in water. Fairly early substitutes (pouring, sometimes sprinkling, of water on the head) were recognized in circumstances of a shortage of water or principally on the sick bed where immersion was not practicable. Baptism of young children occurred when there was danger of death, but this did not become a common practice in absence of an emergency until the fifth or sixth century. The normal practice for centuries was an immersion of penitent believers upon a confession of faith.[2]

CONCLUSION

As his name is called on us, in baptism we call on his name. Baptism is an act of "calling on the name of the Lord" (Acts 22: 16; see 2:21). It is expressive of obedience and surrender. Baptism is always in a context of faith and repentance (Heb. 10:22; Mk. 16:16; Acts 8:37; Col. 2:12; Acts 2:38). It is an oath of allegiance (so the possible meaning of the "answer" in 1 Pet. 3:21) which excludes other loyalties. Just as it is faith and repentance which give baptism its initial validity, so it is faith and repentance which continue to give baptism its saving power in the Christian life. Some seem to think that at baptism God takes care of past sins, and from that point one is on his own. But the benefits of baptism continue to flow forward to cover the entirety of one's life in Christ, that is, if faith and repentance continue to characterize one's life. Faith and repentance give baptism its significance, and they continue to enable one to appropriate forgiveness after baptism.

The New Testament teaches that baptism has real value but that it draws that value from the command of God and the presence

---

2   Everett Ferguson, *Baptism in the Early Church: History, Theology, and Liturgy in the First Five Centuries* (Grand Rapids: Eerdmans, 2009), provides a comprehensive study of the New Testament practice, its background, and later developments.

of faith. Baptism is a symbol, as the ancient world understood a symbol, that accomplishes what it symbolizes. Specifically it is an act of prophetic-symbolism. The prophets' symbolic actions were God's word in deed (cf. Jer. 27–28; Ezek. 4). They not only declared God's action, but because God's word is true those acts actually set in motion its fulfillment. But prophecy was conditional. God's promises were dependent on the faith and repentance of the people. In a similar way baptism is the act appointed by God to convey the blessings of Christ to his people.

REVIEW QUESTIONS

1. Describe different views of baptism held in Christendom.

2. What gives baptism its saving power according to the New Testament?

3. What is the significance of the Great Commission for the doctrine of baptism and for the church?

4. Relate the word "power" to the resurrection, preaching, and baptism.

5. How does baptism as "death, burial, and resurrection" relate to membership in the church?

6. What characteristics of the Messianic Age are bestowed at baptism?

7. When and how is one incorporated into the church? Who is the real administrator of baptism?

8. How does baptism relate to the continuation of the Christian life?

9. What does baptism "in the name of Christ" mean? Consult Bible dictionaries and commentaries for additional help.

10. Does baptism only bring forgiveness of past sins, or does it have continuing significance for one's relation to God?

Lesson 6

LIFE IN THE CHURCH

God "chose us in him...that we should be holy."
(Ephesians 1:4)

BAPTISM AND THE CHRISTIAN LIFE

MANY OF THE PASSAGES CONCERNING baptism discussed in the preceding lesson occur in contexts of ethical instruction to Christians (Rom. 6:1–11; 1 Cor. 12:13; Eph. 5:26–27; Col. 2:12–13). The New Testament epistles taught Christians the meaning and implications of the baptism by which they had been previously incorporated into the people of Christ (Acts 2:38; 18:8). Baptism has a definite meaning for Christians because baptism sets the standard for the Christian life. Baptism represents the principles governing Christian ethical conduct—death to sin (Rom. 6:2–3), gift of the Holy Spirit (1 Cor. 6:11), new life in Christ (Tit. 3:4; 2 Cor. 5:17). Becoming a Christian determines what it means to be a Christian.

Christians treat "one another and all" (1 Thess. 3:12) in a certain way because they are related to Christ in a special way: they are in Christ (Gal. 3:27) and Christ is among them (Col. 1:27). Therefore, the Christian's task is to become what in Christ he is (see Lesson 3). This is the essence of the Christian's life: to live out what has been given to him in his baptism.

One scholar has suggested that Philippians 2:5 be rendered, "Live as befits your standing in the church of Christ." The church is the sphere in which the new life in Christ is lived out. The church provides the framework for Christian ethical activity. The church is a part of God's redemptive plan, not only as the means of communicating the saving gospel, but also as the place where the redeemed life is actualized (Eph. 4:1–6, 11–32).

Many sermons have been preached on "how to identify the church of the Lord." An important point in such sermons should be the manner of life of the members. There are distinguishing qualities to the Christian life. That life is conditioned by a particular relationship with God which has been established in Christ.

KNOWING GOD

The idea of "knowing God" occurs frequently in discussions of moral concerns in the New Testament. Christian conduct is grounded in who and what God is.

The same associations recur in several passages on ethical conduct: 1 Peter 1:13–22; Ephesians 4:17–24; 1 Thessalonians 4:1–12. We select a few for special mention. These themes had been common in Jewish writings against the Gentiles and are continued in the New Testament. They may be summarized as follows: a false view of God led to a false worship, and this in turn led to a false conduct.

In the Old Testament it was the Gentile world that knew not God (Jer. 10:25). When Israel, to whom a knowledge of God had been entrusted, was disobedient, this was described as not knowing God (Isa. 1:3; Jer. 8:7). Theophanies (manifestations of God) made people aware of the holiness of God and in contrast the sinfulness of human life. One of the clearest and best known is the experience of Isaiah in Isaiah 6:1–13. In the present dispensation people come to know God through Christ (2 Cor. 4:4–6; Eph. 4:20–24), and this knowledge is fuller.

Ignorance of God issued in immorality (1 Pet. 1:14; 1 Thess. 4:5; Eph. 4:17–19). Consider especially Romans 1:18–32 where the sins of the Gentile world are attributed to a sinful refusal to accept the knowledge of God available to human beings.

Immorality and idolatry are closely related in these passages, as they are often in the Bible. One's view of God determines one's ethics. Therefore, associated with the ignorance of God is notice of the "futile" or "vain" things of the pagan world (1 Pet. 1:18; Eph. 4:17).

On the positive side, to know God is to learn his will. And to learn God's will has ethical and moral influence (1 Thess. 4:9). The passages referring to the "will of God" in the New Testament are frequently in contexts where ethical implications are in the forefront (Rom. 2:18; 12:2; Eph. 5:17; 6:6; 1 Thess. 4:3; Heb. 13:21; 1 Pet. 2:15; 4:2). This will has now been revealed through Christ and his spokesmen (Eph. 4:20–21; 1 Thess. 4:1–2).

Knowledge of God thus becomes the standard of ethical conduct because of the nature of God. A word which comes to the forefront in such discussions is "holy." God is a holy God ("the holy One of Israel" is the common designation of God in Isaiah), and therefore his people are to be holy. A good place to begin is the text verse of Leviticus, "You shall be holy; for I the Lord your God am holy" (Lev. 19:2), which introduces various moral instructions. The character of the people was to be determined by the nature of their God. This holiness finds expression in personal and social ethics. The context of Leviticus 19 is evident in several passages in the New Testament, and 19:2 itself is quoted in Peter's ethical instructions to Gentile converts (1 Pet. 1:16).

The servant of God confesses God's holiness; that holiness controls his life. This control is not exercised in some artificial way, but because of the desire to please him (1 Thess. 4:1) and because of the new relationship established (Eph. 5:3). Thus Christian conduct is the response of those redeemed by Christ (1 Pet. 1:16–18; Eph. 4:32–5:2). One does what he does because of God. Even in social sins, the transgression is not so much against human beings as it is against God (1 Thess. 4:8). A sin against one's own body is a sin against God, because even the body of the Christian belongs to God (1 Cor. 6:18–20).

SANCTIFICATION OF THE SPIRIT

When one comes to the knowledge of God, it is through the revelation of the Spirit (1 Cor. 2:6–13). When one responds to the words of the Spirit and is baptized (1 Pet. 1:22), he receives the Spirit of God (1 Thess. 4:18). This Spirit is the Spirit of holiness (Rom. 1:4)—the *Holy* Spirit (1 Cor. 6:19; Eph. 4:30). The Spirit participates in the nature of God. Thus the Spirit's work in the life of the Christian is sanctification (2 Thess. 2:13; 1 Pet. 1:2). Sanctification brings one to become like God. This is not a product of unaided human effort, but it is the achievement of the Spirit.

The "process" of sanctification is a matter of continuous growth in the Christian life. It reaches its consummation only in the world to come. At times sanctification is identified with the reception of the Spirit at baptism as a definite past act (1 Cor. 6:11; 1 Thess. 4:7; Heb. 10:10). At other times, sanctification is the present process of the Spirit's working (1 Thess. 4:3; Rom. 6:19; Heb. 12:14). Sometimes sanctification is placed only at the end as an eschatological (related to last things) accomplishment (1 Thess. 3:13; 5:23).

Very often the non-Christian will do the same acts as the Christian. But there is a difference between a Christian and a non-Christian doing the same thing. It is the difference between a good, ethical act and the quality of sanctification. The Christian does what he does, not just because it is an ethical act or the "right thing" to do or the expedient thing to do, or whatever motivates the non-Christian. He does what he does *because he knows God and God's will and because of the Spirit's sanctification.* Thus the Christian's conduct has a different reason or basis and a different value to it.

The qualities and activities of the Christian life are the fruit, or the product of the working of the Spirit in the life of God's people (Gal. 5:16–26; Rom. 8:1–17; Eph. 3:16). The gifts of the Spirit extend beyond supernatural manifestations (1 Cor. 12–14). Indeed the greatest gifts of the Spirit—faith, hope and love (1 Cor. 12:31–14:1)—are available to every Christian. These qualities which are the "fruit of the Spirit" are the consequences of one's knowing God and receiving his Spirit.

LOVE OF CHRIST

Thus far we have considered the basic doctrinal grounding of Christian morality. Now we may take a look at the basic principle governing the application of this conduct, which is grounded in the holiness of God. The ruling Christian ethical principle is love (*agapē*), the self-giving attitude that wills the best for another. It is noteworthy how often the Spirit and love come together in the same contexts (Rom. 5:5; 15:30; Gal 5:22; Col. 1:8). Love is the highest product of the working of God's Spirit. God is love (1 John 4:8). "We love because he first loved us"—God commands a service of love, and he gives the love that empowers the service (1 John 4:19). This love is toward God and people (Matt. 22:36–40), and it is indeed absolute (there is no object in 1 John 4:19). The motivation for conduct is the will of God: for this reason one loves (1 Thess. 4:9).

Love triumphed over law in God's treatment of human beings (1 Pet. 4:18–19; Rom. 5:6–11; 1 John 4:9–11). Even so, love triumphs over law in our conduct. Law as a principle cannot change the heart, impart the power to keep its prescriptions, or bring peace of mind. On the other hand, the Christian does not despise law (1 Tim. 1:8; Rom. 7:12). He neither ignores rules and regulations, nor is he their slave. Rules may preserve a principle and guide its application, but they can never encompass it. At times one may have to act in such a way as to break the rules in order to be faithful to a principle (as one who stops on the way to church to render assistance at an accident and so misses services), but one should always be sure that he is acting on principle and not on whim when he does so. It is easy to deceive ourselves as to our real motives. Thus specific requirements are necessary guides to conduct. The spirit that infuses their observance is the spirit of love.

THE CHALLENGE OF CHRISTIAN ETHICS

From what has been studied it is clear that Christian ethics is something more than just "doing good" or performing lists of duties. There are specific things a Christian will not do, as the many lists of vices in the New Testament indicate (Col. 3:5–9; Eph. 4:24–31; 5:3–5; 1 Tim. 1:9–11; 2 Tim. 3:2–5). And there are positive specifics of Christian conduct spelled out in certain passages as the inspired authors apply Christian principles to particular situations. But the primary thrust of New Testament ethical teaching has to do with qualities of life. Christian living is much more challenging than a list of "do's and don'ts." Also, it allows no place for smugness or complacency in thinking that one has lived up to the requirements. But to deny the validity of reducing the Christian life to a list does not make Christian living easier, for one can never be satisfied with where he is in spiritual growth while he follows the leading of the Spirit of the living God. There is an openness to the future in Christian ethics. It demands the very best in one.

This high standard of conduct is involved in one's response to Christ, and it is possible because of that response. The Christian life is both a gift and a task. God through his Spirit gives not only the demands but also the power of living the transformed life. Human beings do not have to do it alone; we have divine assistance. Part of this divine assistance comes from the support of the redeemed community. One's new life is lived in the church. It is life in the community of those who also have shared the grace of God in Christ. Part of God's plan for people is that they should grow up into the fullness of salvation. In order to do this, association with other fellow Christians in the community of faith is essential.

REVIEW QUESTIONS

1. What relationship does baptism sustain to Christian living?

2. In what way is the church important for Christian living?

3. Give some of the principal New Testament passages discussing Christian ethical conduct.

4. How is "knowing God" important for Christian conduct?

5. What is the result of not knowing God?

6. What quality of God determines the morality of his people?

7. Discuss the Biblical teaching on sanctification.

8. Look up passages where the Spirit forms the standard of morality.

9. Why does the Christian love?

10. Discuss the place of rules in Christian living. How does Christian living transcend mere rule-keeping?

Lesson 7

FELLOWSHIP OF THE CHURCH

"Called into the fellowship of his Son"
(1 Corinthians 1:9)

ONE OF THE RICHLY MEANINGFUL aspects of the Christian life, and one that lies close to the basic meaning of the church, is the fellowship of the saints in Christ. The idea of fellowship emphasizes the corporateness (group relationship) of the church and calls attention to the sense of belonging and participation.

Fellowship translates the word *koinōnia*, which means joint participation, having in common, communion, sharing, mutuality. The prominence of this concept in the New Testament is indicated not only by the group of words related to *koinōnia*, but by the large number of compounds formed with the preposition "with," which suggests a close association (these are especially frequent in Philippians). A noteworthy class of these compounds are those nouns translated in English "fellow worker," "fellow servant," "fellow disciple," "fellow citizen," and the like.

FELLOWSHIP WITH CHRIST

In the days of his flesh Jesus called people to follow him and become part of his fellowship (Matt 4:18–22). He called them to himself. They were to learn of him and take his yoke upon themselves (Matt. 11:25–30). There was nothing impersonal about that call, and though we no longer know him "according to the flesh," his call is no less personal today (2 Cor. 5:16–20). Jesus calls people to become his disciples and to learn what he teaches (Matt. 28:19–20). The initiative still comes from God, who calls people into the fellowship of his Son (1 Cor. 1:9; cf. Heb. 3:1).

This fellowship is based on a proclamation. God calls through the gospel in order that one may obtain the glory of Jesus (2 Thess. 2:14; cf. 1 Thess. 1:4–5). In its essence the message through which God in Christ calls people has Jesus himself as its very content (1 John 1:1–4). One not only learns of Christ, but in the message is to learn Christ himself (Eph. 4:20–21). In this way it is still Christ himself who calls people to himself (John 12:32).

To understand fellowship properly, therefore, one must begin by seeing it as something created by God in Christ. It is not all of our own doing. By responding to God's call (1 Thess. 2:12) people become sharers in the divine nature (2 Pet. 1:3–4). When people receive the message of Christ and become committed, they receive Christ and begin a life in which they are to become more like him (Col. 2:6; cf. 2 Cor. 5:17; 6:14; 7:1). Now their life is hid with Christ in God (Col. 3:3). Their hearts and minds are kept in Christ (Phil. 4:7), for in him they share a renewal of the mind (Rom. 12:2) and experience his peace in their hearts (Col. 3:15). They have dedicated themselves so completely to their Master that the goal of their life is that Christ be formed in them (Gal. 4:19) so that it is no longer they who live, but Christ who lives in them (Gal. 2:20).

Those who are "called according to his purpose" (Rom. 8:28) have been "set free" (Rom. 8:2) at God's initiative (Rom. 8:3). By setting their minds "on the Spirit" they now have "life and peace" (Rom. 8:6), having become "children of God,…heirs of God and fellow heirs with Christ" (Rom. 8:16–17). Their lives have thus become dominated by their fellowship with Christ.

FELLOWSHIP OF DISCIPLES

Basically, Christian fellowship is God given, not man chosen. Christians have fellowship with one another because they have fellowship with God in Christ. They are "one" with each other because they are "one" with him (John 17:20–23). Christian fellowship is a communion with Jesus Christ shared by fellow Christians. This communion with Christ is the ground for the corporate life which exhibits him. A common fellowship with the Lord produces a fellowship of those who share it.

As people are drawn to the cross they find that they are not alone: they are in company with others who have had the same experience. The fellowship with other believers is already established by God; it is a part of that which is "given" on entering into fellowship with Christ. One's task is to work out in a practical way this God given fellowship, to maintain the "unity of the Spirit in the bond of peace" (Eph. 4:3). Human fraternity is based on liking each other and choosing to be together. Christians are already together in Christ, therefore they choose to like each other. They become united together by their life in the Lord. They are a community that comes into existence and continues to exist by virtue of its relationship with Christ. Relationships which would ordinarily alienate people from each other are submerged, in sharing the fellowship of Christ (Philemon; Gal. 3:28; Col. 3:11).

The basis of fellowship in the church thus is found in a common salvation by the same Savior, and in a common loyalty to one Lord (Eph. 4:4–5). All spiritual blessings are jointly shared (Rom. 15:27), and expressive of all of these is the joint sharing of faith (Philem. 6). There is no possession of Christians more precious than their faith. A concrete expression of this common faith is the "right hand of fellowship" (Gal. 2:9).

Christians are joint partakers of the Holy Spirit (Phil. 2:1). The one Spirit is one of the bases of Christian unity (Eph. 4:4). The one Holy Spirit of God introduces one into the fellowship of the church at baptism (1 Cor. 12:13), distributes a variety of gifts for the service of the whole church (1 Cor. 12:4–7), and is the source of spiritual nourishment and refreshment in the Christian life (1 Cor. 12:13).

The unifying factor in Christian fellowship is the love which Christ demonstrated for us (Col. 3:14). When Christians so understand the nature of that love that it transforms them not only as individuals but as a fellowship it becomes a sign and proof of their discipleship (John 13:35; cf. Acts 2:43–47). They have fellowship with God and enjoy his continual cleansing (1 John 1:5–7). On the basis of God, Christ, and the Holy Spirit a human community is established (2 Cor. 13:14; cf. Acts 2:42).

SHARED ACTIVITIES

This corporate fellowship which is created as Christians share the life in Christ is given a more clearly defined character by specific expressions of its sense of community.

In her worship the church is led by Christ (Col. 3:15–17). Thus in the participation or fellowship in the Lord's supper the church participates in Christ, and this participation in return results in a communion of believers (1 Cor. 10:16–17).

As the church proclaims Christ, her members share in the gospel when they support the preaching (Phil. 1:3–8). This fellowship is exercised not only in providing support for those who preach, but also in a willingness to accept it as an offering to God (Phil. 4:14–19). Fellowship may involve the practical concerns of preaching, such as financial arrangements and the agreement among Christians as to special areas of responsibility (Gal. 2:9–10), but it is never merely a practical matter. Christians seek to have this fellowship for God's sake and to be fellow sharers in the truth (3 John 6–8). When they preach they do so not only as partners with each other or as messengers of the church, they do so also as the glory of Christ (2 Cor. 8:23; cf. Col. 1:27–28).

Fellowship is also expressed through the use of the Christian's possessions. The attitude expressed by the author of Hebrews 13:16 is one basic to the whole New Testament: "Do not neglect to do good and to share what you have, for such sacrifices are pleasing to God." Thus the needs of the saints provide an opportunity to have fellowship with them (Rom. 12:13; 2 Cor. 8:4). It is not only an opportunity to alleviate hardship, but becomes an occasion by which God may be glorified (2 Cor. 9:13). For this practical meeting of needs to become true fellowship, it must not only be given in the right manner, but it must also be received as an act of fellowship (Rom. 15:26, 30–31). In the original the words for both "contribute" and "take a part" in these passages is fellowship.

THE REFUSAL OF FELLOWSHIP

It is a characteristic of true fellowship that it wants to embrace all men and women who share in Christ. Fellowship is a natural part of the Christian life we are to seek. Many passages speak to the precious nature of Christian fellowship (1 Thess. 2:8–11, 20; 3 John 3, 4; Phil. 4:1–3; Acts 20:36–38).

Precisely because this sharing in Christ is so important, it is something to be cherished and kept pure. It has value only if it represents a better way, a higher life. To continue in the fellowship with the Father who calls us into it, we must continue to obey his commandments (1 John 2:3–6) and must hold to what we have heard from the beginning (1 John 2:24–25; Heb. 3:14). Since God establishes the fellowship in Christ, unless our concerns are congruent with his actions in regard to fellowship we do not bring into effect fellowship but only a certain kind of "togetherness."

Christians are not to share in others' sins (1 Tim. 5:22). By accepting into its fellowship someone who does not have God in his life the church would share in his wicked work (2 John 9–11). In her desire to share her communion with Christ with others, the church yet knows that she cannot share in the unfruitful works of darkness, but that she is to expose them (Eph. 5:11). For that reason she is on her guard against iniquity and darkness, refusing to become like them by having fellowship with them (2 Cor. 6:14). The early church used "letters of recommendation" to protect themselves in this regard (Acts 18:27; 2 Cor. 3:1–2).

WITHDRAWING FELLOWSHIP

Because her fellowship is an index of her real character, the church must also be concerned to withdraw herself from elements that are foreign to her. One purpose of withdrawing fellowship is, therefore, to preserve the church's identity (1 Cor. 5:6–8, 12–13). As a community of believers she must be so thoroughly the Lord's that in her fellowship she witnesses to him. When the reflection of Christ by the church is damaged by someone, the church must withdraw from him. Such a person is one who refuses to submit himself to the life of Christ, whether in his moral life (1 Cor. 5), or by his rejection of Christ's teachings (Rom. 16:17–18; cf. 2 Thess. 3:6–15), or by his general conduct in the body of Christ (Titus 3:10–11; 2 Thess. 3:11–12).

But withdrawal can only have real meaning if the church's fellowship is real. If her fellowship does not have the qualities so far observed, "withdrawal of fellowship" is meaningless, for there is in fact nothing of substance that can be withdrawn. The fellowship of the church must be a reality that can be experienced and seen by Christians and the world. Withdrawal implies a great self-consciousness by the church of her own importance both with respect to her corporate relationship with the Lord and with respect to her relationship with individual Christians. The second purpose for withdrawal is to discipline the one withdrawn from (1 Cor. 5:5; 2 Thess. 3:14). Being made up of concerned brothers and sisters, the church can punish, and also forgive and comfort (2 Thess. 3:15; 2 Cor. 2:6–7). If the self-confidence that makes this disciplining action possible is not to become gross arrogance the church must ever seek to develop the right kind of fellowship, and must see withdrawal in this perspective.

Withdrawal must further take place with the awesome and humbling realization that since the fellowship involved is created by Christ, it can also only be dissolved by him. He not only commands that withdrawal take place and explains how it is to be done (Matt. 18:15–19), but is himself present to lend his authority to it when it is being effected (Matt. 18:20; 1 Cor. 5:4; 2 Thess. 3:6, 12). The church is acting for Christ in this endeavor. As God through Christ calls us to this fellowship, he continues to determine its character.

The withdrawal of fellowship includes refusal of the Lord's supper (Lesson 9). Hence, the withdrawal of fellowship was later called excommunication (the exclusion from communion). The church has no higher or other power of discipline than the exercise of this protection of the boundaries of its membership. It does so in the spirit of exercising what a merciful but holy God would have done.

REVIEW QUESTIONS

1. What is the meaning of the original word which is translated fellowship?

2. Consult a concordance or Bible dictionary for some of the usages of fellowship in the New Testament.

3. How is this fellowship in Christ based on a proclamation?

4. How does the religious usage of the New Testament differ from secular ideas of fellowship? What is the doctrinal grounding of fellowship?

5. Name some of the things jointly shared by Christians? Can you extend the list given in the lesson?

6. How is the contribution of money and goods an expression of fellowship?

7. When should the church refuse to accept one into its fellowship?

8. What individuals are objects of disfellowshipping in the New Testament?

9. What are the purposes of the withdrawal of fellowship?

10. Relate the theme of this lesson to other topics in this series of lessons.

Lesson 8

THE WORSHIP OF THE CHURCH

"In spirit and in truth"
(John 4:24)

ALTHOUGH WORSHIP IS PERFORMED IN private devotions and meditations, in its fullest expression worship is a group act. The church reveals itself as it really is in worship. There may be defects where a church becomes only a worshipping society. True worship, however, will not permit this to happen. One-sided distortions should not blind one to the importance of worship for the life of the church, for in worship the essence of the church is expressed. Throughout Christian history the corporate assembly for worship has appropriately been called a "service." It is not a distinct act of service separate from other acts, but a way of serving God intimately connected with other acts of service.

GOD THE OBJECT

Worship is offered to the glory of God, in Christ, by the Spirit for the edification of the church. The order of this statement is important. God is the object of worship, and worship must be God-centered, not human-centered. Only God is worthy. If one goes to worship for what he can "get out of it," he goes for the wrong reason. One goes to give glory to God. He is drawn by gratitude for what God has done for him in Christ. Spiritual benefits for the individual worshippers certainly result, and the principal means by which the church is built up in the faith is the corporate service of worship. Worship may certainly be an emotional, soul-stirring experience (and this effect should not be despised), but, like happiness, the uplift of worship does not come by "looking for it" but as a by-product of other worthwhile activities.

The doctrinal understanding of worship must be grounded in God. Worship is determined by the nature of God. One of the most profound descriptions of worship is found in John 4:21–24. Since God is Spirit, worship must be in spirit and in truth, that is, it must be spiritual and real (the Greek word for "truth" here suggests "reality"). Worship must be genuine and true. Since God is the creator and sustainer of life, the creature must come before God on God's terms. The basic attitude must be one of humility.

Paul bases his instructions on the corporate conduct of worship in 1 Corinthians 11 on the order of nature established by creation. This provides a doctrinal explanation for the position assigned to women in worship. Women's activity in the church is restricted in public worship but nowhere else (1 Cor. 14:34–36; 1 Tim. 2:11–14 are descriptions of public worship). Subordination in this one sphere is probably due to the nature of worship: it is addressed to the Creator; hence one observes the order of creation—man first, then woman. One comes to God as his Maker, or he does not worship God (Heb. 11:3, 6).

IN CHRIST

The peculiar character of the worship of the church is governed by the fact that it is "in Christ." Christ's body is the new temple (John 2:19). He is "the truth" (John 14:16). The Christian comes to God not only as Creator but as the Father of Jesus Christ. Redemption has given a new relationship with God and a new motivation for worship. Thus Christian worship is distinctively related to the "name of Christ."

The outward acts, or avenues, through which worship is expressed are offered to God through Jesus Christ. It is "in his name," "with respect to him," "out of worship for Christ" that these things are done. In the central and distinctive act of the church's worship, the Lord's supper (to be studied more fully in the next lesson), the relationship to Jesus is obvious. Jesus instituted this act of thanksgiving (Mk. 14:22–25 and parallels). The repetition is a memorial of Jesus, done with reference to him (1 Cor. 11:24, 26). The bread shares the same designation as does the church—his body (Matt. 26:26; Col. 1:18). Participation in the supper is thus a participation (fellowship) in Christ (1 Cor. 10:16–17). In so honoring Christ the Christian honors God, and acknowledges God's action in Christ for his salvation.

The other actions of worship, which had been engaged in by God's people before the coming of Christ, now have a new focus in Christ, expressed by the formula "in his name." Thus prayer—whether of adoration, confession, thanksgiving, or supplication—is now offered "to God, through Christ, in the Holy Spirit," to summarize one of the formulas of the ancient church. (See 1 Tim. 2:1–5; John 14:13–14; Rom. 8:26–27) Prayer is an act of the whole congregation. When one speaks for the people to God, he assumes only a slightly less solemn task and should make little less preparation than the one who speaks for God to the people. The members of the congregation ratify the prayer as their own by the solemn pronunciation of the "Amen," which means "may it be so," "this is our prayer too" (1 Cor. 14:16).

Singing is also to God "in his name" (Eph. 5:19–20; Col. 3:16–17). "Psalms, hymns, and spiritual songs," although having slightly different connotations, appear to have been used without precise differentiation. Here especially is it important not to confuse aesthetics with worship. Nevertheless, the songs chosen should conform to the spiritual nature of worship and emphasize the objective character of God's salvation.

Jesus is the motive and example in our giving (2 Cor. 8:9). The contribution is an offering, a sacrifice (Phil. 4:18; 1 Cor. 16:1–3; 2 Cor. 9:12). It is one of the principal expressions of fellowship in Christ. Thus it has important doctrinal associations, and it is noteworthy that Scripture does not appeal to practical considerations in encouraging one to give (in 2 Cor. 8–9 Paul does not even urge the fact that the Jerusalem Christians are poor and need help), but always places teaching on giving in a religious context.

Christ is the essential content of the Scripture readings and preaching of the church (Lk. 24:44–45; Acts 8:35; and note the sermons in Acts). Christians read all of the Bible in terms of Christ. Their teaching is all related to him. Preaching in a worship service ideally is expository of the contents of Scripture, for on this occasion the word of God is spoken to human beings and applied to their needs.

BY THE HOLY SPIRIT

The Holy Spirit, who is the Spirit of Christ, inspires and guides Christian worship and presents that worship to God (1 Cor. 12:3b; 14:15; Rom. 8:26–27; Eph. 5:18–19). Worship is "in the Spirit." This is what makes it spiritual. The Spirit unites believers in the one body of Christ and brings their worship to Christ and God.

EDIFICATION

Biblical religion is almost unique among world religions in placing the reading of Scripture and teaching and preaching based on them in the context of worship (1 Tim. 4:13; Col. 3:15–17). Paul makes edification of the group the criterion for determining what is acceptable in Christian worship and how it is to be carried on (1 Cor. 14:1–26).

ELEMENTS OF WORSHIP

The principal concern in worship often has been how to do it, not what it is. Thus there has been more emphasis on the acts of worship than on what is done through these acts. It may help the doctrinal study of the worship of the church to list some of the aspects or elements of worship. It is not expected that this will be an exhaustive list, or that all will be equally significant. With these elements portraying the nature of worship will be indicated the avenues through which they may be expressed.

Praise, or adoration, is certainly one of the important aspects of worship. "We become like what we worship" describes the impact on us of adoration. Praise may be conveyed through reading Scriptures of praise, in the wording of the prayers, through the preached word, and in singing hymns of praise.

Thanksgiving is another prominent element in Christian worship. It is grounded in the very nature of the believers' response to God in Christ. Thanksgiving may be expressed in reading Scriptures of thanksgiving, in the prayers, in the songs of gratitude, and preeminently in the Lord's supper (see next lesson).

Remembrance has a large place in Biblical religion, which is a historical religion. It has been said that "it is the forgetful man who does not worship." One reason the reading of the Bible has such a large place in both the public and private devotions of Christians is that the Scriptures remind us of God and the history of his people who have witnessed the outpouring of his blessings and judgments. Remembrance not only includes past acts but also looks forward to the fulfillment of God's promises. Besides Scripture reading, preaching and especially the Lord's supper are acts in which remembrance takes an essential part.

Sacrifice or offering has always, everywhere been an expression of worship. Sacrifice has been purified in its motives through the teachings of the Bible, for the man of God pays his vows and makes his offerings not to appease God or to win him over for a favor, but to express a dedication of himself to the fulfillment of God's will and the love of his heart to humankind. Sacrifice has been spiritualized in the worship of the church. The Christian's sacrifice is offered through song, prayer, the Lord's supper, and the contribution of money and goods.

The *confession* of sin and the confession of faith are related aspects of worship. Their common element is the recognition of the holiness and mercy of God. This recognition calls forth the profession of faith and the acknowledgement of sin. Individual verbal statements, prayers, songs, and Scripture readings are means of presenting confessions.

Teaching, as observed above, is a distinctive feature of Biblical worship. God is honored as his people are edified and instructed. Teaching may be done by singing, reading the Bible, and especially by preaching.

Requests also pertain to the worship of the church. What distinguishes the petitions of Christian worship from the mere begging of those who know not the God of the Bible is the larger perspective in which the petitions and intercessions of Christian prayer are set. All is included in the comprehensive petition, "Thy will be done." There are prayer songs, and prayer Scriptures as well as spoken prayers. These are different ways of voicing the requests of the people of God.

LATER DEVELOPMENTS

The earliest Christian writings after the New Testament reflect the same activities in the Christian assembly: Scripture reading, preaching, prayer, Lord's supper, and giving (see especially Justin Martyr, *1 Apology* 67, about the year 150).[3] Soon the leadership in worship was limited to the clergy, and eventually the role of the people became more that of observers than of participants. In time written prayers and orders of service became not simply guides for the leaders in the service but set forms routinely followed according to a church calendar. This development served to preserve correct doctrine but limited spontaneity and flexibility.

The songs of the early church were unaccompanied by instrumental music. In the Middle Ages organ music was introduced into the service in the western Catholic Church, but the eastern Orthodox Churches maintained unaccompanied vocal music.[4]

---

3   Quoted in Everett Ferguson, *Early Christians Speak*, 3rd edition (Abilene: ACU Press, 1999), 79–80.

4   Everett Ferguson, *A Cappella Music in the Public Worship of the Church*, 4th edition (Abilene: Desert Willow, 2013).

REVIEW QUESTIONS

1. When is the church most truly itself?

2. What determines the nature of worship?

3. What are the basic attitudes with which one must come before God in worship?

4. How has Christ transformed worship?

5. In what way may it be said that Christian worship is performed in the Spirit?

6. What criterion of acceptable worship did Paul set before the Corinthians?

7. Distinguish acts of worship from elements of worship.

8. Name some of the elements of worship suggested in this lesson.

9. What other elements would you add to this list?

10. Which should be emphasized more, the outward acts or the essential elements of worship? Are there certain outward acts which are more appropriate for the expression of the essential elements of Christian worship than others?

Lesson 9

THE LORD'S SUPPER

"This is my body."
(Matthew 26:26)

THE NEW TESTAMENT USES THE word "body" in reference to Jesus in four different senses: (1) the physical body of his incarnation (Heb. 10:5; Lk. 23:52); (2) the glorified body of his resurrection (Phil. 3:21); (3) the spiritual body of his church (Col. 1:18; Eph. 1:23); and (4) the bread of the Lord's Supper (Matt. 26:26). Each of these usages has bearing on the nature of the church. The Son of God became flesh and blood (cf. John 1:14; 19:34; Heb. 2:14) so that by his death and resurrection he might redeem a new people of God (Col. 1:18–20; Phil. 2:5–10; Acts 20:28). These people will some day share the likeness of his glorification (Phil. 3:21; 1 Cor. 15:44; 1 John 3:2). Paul unites concepts (3) and (4) when he declares that by partaking of the one bread Christians become the one body of Christ (1 Cor. 10:16–17). But first the Spirit at baptism must incorporate them into the body of Christ (1 Cor. 12:13). Receiving spiritual nourishment from the Lord (John 6:35–40, 47–58, 63), they are transformed into his glory (2 Cor. 3:18).

The Lord's supper, above all other acts of worship, is expressive of what the church is. There are a number of ideas associated with the Lord's supper which are relevant for the doctrine of the church.

THANKSGIVING

At the institution of the Lord's supper Jesus "gave thanks" (the verb form of *eucharistia*, thanksgiving). This is also the meaning of "blessed" (Mk. 14:22). It was the customary Jewish practice at the beginning of a meal to take bread, say a prayer, and break it. Jesus had often done this in his meals with his disciples (Mk. 6:41) so that Jesus was recognized by his characteristic manner of doing this (Lk. 24:30, 35). Thus the Lord's supper was known in the early church as the "breaking of bread" (Acts 2:42; 20:7). At the Jewish Passover there was also a "cup of blessing" (cf. 1 Cor. 10:16) as part of the meal in commemoration of the escape from Egypt. Jesus took these familiar gestures and on the night of the Last Supper endowed them with a new meaning.

When we repeat Jesus' actions we also "give thanks" to God. The material elements serve to remind us of all of God's gifts. But at this moment we are particularly mindful of the gifts that pertain to salvation.

The Lord's supper is the church's great act of thanksgiving for all that pertains to its life in the Lord.

MEMORIAL

Paul cites Jesus' words of institution as containing the command "do this in remembrance of me" (1 Cor. 11:24, 26). The phrase is literally "do this memorial (*anamnēsis*) of me."

The commemorative aspect of the Lord's Supper is made clearer by reference to Jewish practices. Jesus' words "This is my body" may be related to the words of Exodus 12:11, "It is the Lord's Passover." When the Jews celebrated the Passover memorial (*mnemosunon*) (Ex. 12:14), there was more than just a remembrance of a past event. Each Jew who celebrated the Passover became himself a participant in the Exodus event. The Mishnah enjoined, "In every generation a man must so regard himself as if he came forth himself out of Egypt." The deliverance from bondage became his own experience. Thus, instead of calling the past to mind, the past was brought into the present and its benefits made operative.

Paul further says that in raising this memorial of Jesus we are "showing forth his death" (1 Cor. 11:26). In the Lord's supper there is a portraying, a showing forth, a re-enactment. Here another Old Testament concept will be helpful in appreciating the significance of what Jesus did at the Last Supper. In likening the familiar actions of breaking bread and pouring out the fruit of the vine to his body and blood Jesus was establishing a point of prophetic symbolism. Jesus' flesh was broken and given for humankind (John 19:34; 20:25–29; 1 Cor 11:24) and his blood was poured out for the remission of sins (Matt. 26:28). Since the symbol partakes of the reality being enacted, when we repeat the action of Jesus, we bring the benefits of his death once more into our lives. We participate in his sacrifice (1 Cor. 10:16).

COVENANT

It was the sacrifice of Christ that brought forgiveness of sins and established a new covenant between God and humanity (Heb. 8:6–9:26). Jesus declared that "this is my blood of the covenant" (Matt. 26:28). The Old Covenant was inaugurated by sacrifice, the sprinkling of the blood of the covenant, and the eating of a covenant meal (Ex. 24:3–11). For Christians the eating of the Lord's supper is an act of renewing covenant allegiance to the Lord. This is a relationship which excludes all other religious loyalties (1 Cor. 10:21). The covenant relationship is one of close communion with the Lord. The church is the people of the new covenant who have a new meal.

FELLOWSHIP

The Lord's Supper is also called by Paul a fellowship or communion (*koinōnia*) with the body and blood of the Lord (1 Cor. 10:16–17; see Lesson 7). Christians meet around the Lord's table (1 Cor. 10:21). They eat the "Lord's supper" (1 Cor. 11:20). He invites, and the purpose in coming together is to break bread with him. Table fellowship was full of rich associations of closeness in the Biblical world. Jesus is spiritually present when his people meet in his name.

The passage in 1 Corinthians 10:14–21 points out that eating at idol temples established a communion with demons. Likewise eating of the sacrificial offerings in Judaism made the participants partners of the altar. When Christians eat the bread and drink the cup, they are participating in Christ's body and blood, that is they are sharing in his life and the benefits of that life.

This fellowship is not only with the risen Christ. It is also with one another. We have unity through our allegiance to a common Lord. It is our fellowship with Christ which establishes the fellowship one with another. A concrete expression of our accepting one another is our sharing in the Lord's supper. Communion shows one's participation in the church, for the church is the body of Christ (1 Cor. 12:12). Eating of the "one loaf" makes the participants "one body" in Christ (1 Cor. 10:17). It is only in the one body that we receive the benefits of Christ's death (cf. Eph. 2:16).

MESSIANIC BANQUET

The showing forth of the Lord's death in the supper is "until he comes" (1 Cor. 11:26). The Lord's supper points back to the cross and provides a present fellowship. It further proclaims a future event. Indeed the predominant note of the supper is joyful expectation, for it is not just a crucified Christ who is remembered but a living Lord. The present fellowship is a guarantee and anticipation of a fuller fellowship yet to be enjoyed.

Part of the Jewish eschatological hope was set forth in terms of God's banquet for his people (Isa. 25:6; Lk. 13:29). This provides the background for the banquet parables recorded by Luke (14:1–24), and may be behind the reference to the "marriage supper of the Lamb" (Rev. 19:9). More directly to the point, Jesus at the Last Supper spoke of eating and drinking in the Kingdom of God (Matt. 26:29; Lk. 22:16, 18). In the Lord's supper we anticipate the blessings of the end time. Here is an eschatological act, which shows the church's character as the people who partake of God's eschatological gifts.

Not only does the Lord's supper bring the past into the present, it brings the future into the present. Here we see the church as set between the center (the cross) and the consummation (the coming again) of history.

> And thus that dark betrayal-night,
> With the last advent we unite,
> By one blest chain of loving rite,
> Until He come![5]

SACRIFICE

Christ has made his sacrifice once for all (Heb. 10:10). The church is a living continuation of that sacrifice. The Lord's supper is a reminder that we live by the cross. The resurrection gives assurance that there is power in the sacrificial life. Worshippers ate of the sacrificial animal in Old Testament times. In the Lord's supper there is a spiritual participation in Christ's body and blood and the benefits of that sacrifice (1 Cor. 10:16–22).

Not only do we continue a participation in the Lord's sacrifice. We make our own offering here. All worship is an act of sacrifice—the rational sacrifice of praise and thanksgiving (Heb. 13:15). The Lord's supper as the church's central distinctive act of worship is its great moment of self-sacrifice to the God who has redeemed it.

LORD'S DAY

It may or may not be significant that the Greek adjective derived from the word for Lord (*kuriakos*, meaning "of or pertaining to the Lord," from *kurios*) occurs in the New Testament only twice—in reference to the Lord's supper (1 Cor. 11:20) and

5   George Rawson, "*By Christ redeemed, in Christ restored,*" words by Rawson in 5 verses, 1857 (see nccofc.org.au); added to Arthur H. D. Troyte's Chant, No. 1, in 1860. Fourth verse of the original quoted here.

the Lord's day (Rev. 1:10). The early church met on the first day of the week to partake of the Lord's supper (Acts 20:7). This continued to be the practice of the ancient church, and one of its usual designations for the first day continued to be Lord's day. The Lord's supper and the Lord's day belong together. Both are peculiarly Christ's, and that which unites them is the resurrection.

The first day of the week was the day of the resurrection (Mk. 16:1–10; Lk. 24:1; John 20:1). The Jews kept the Sabbath in memory of the deliverance from Egyptian bondage (Deut. 5:13–15). For Christians the first day of the week has special meaning and significance: it is their day of deliverance from the bondage of sin. On that day Christ broke the bars of death. On that day the Christian celebrates the supper of his Lord as a memorial of the death and resurrection, of forgiveness and the new life. The special meaning of the first day as the day of the resurrection gives doctrinal significance to it as the day of worship and celebration of the Lord's supper.

LATER DEVELOPMENTS

In the period after the New Testament some writers began to view the Lord's supper not just as a sacrifice of thanksgiving but as a sacrifice of atonement. The real presence of Christ at the Lord's supper was emphasized and increasingly given a bodily identification with the elements so that the bread and fruit of the vine were understood literally as the body and blood of Christ. Thus was laid the basis for the medieval doctrine of transubstantiation, which was a philosophical explanation of how the elements were transformed from bread and wine into the body and blood while retaining their physical appearance. These developments were without warrant in the New Testament texts but testify to the central importance the communion had to Christian worship so that there was this theological reflection on what was done.[6]

---

6   Everett Ferguson, *Early Christians Speak*, 3rd edition (Abilene: ACU Press, 1999), 91–123.

REVIEW QUESTIONS

1. In what senses is the word "body" used with reference to Jesus?

2. Is it correct to speak of the Lord's supper as "the central act of Christian worship"? Give reasons for both an affirmative and a negative answer.

3. Name some aspects of the Lord's supper which relate to the meaning of the church.

4. How does the Lord's supper show the nature of the church?

5. What does the word "eucharist" literally mean? "*Anamnēsis*"? "*Koinōnia*"?

6. What Old Testament concepts and practices bear on the understanding of the Lord's supper? In what way?

7. What is meant when one says that the Lord's supper is an eschatological act?

8. Is there an appropriate way in which the Lord's supper may be spoken of as a sacrifice?

9. In modern Greek the word for Sunday is *kuriakē* (Lord's' day). What evidence is this for the church's day of worship?

10. Why is the first day of the week important for Christians? What does this say about the partaking of the Lord's supper?

Lesson 10

THE WORK OF THE CHURCH

"Created in Christ Jesus for good works"
(Ephesians 2:10)

GOOD WORKS DO NOT PROCURE human salvation or place God under some kind of obligation to human beings. But saved people work. Christians are in Christ to perform good works (Eph. 2:10). The church continues the ministry of Jesus in the world. The church is his body, in a way an extension of his self into the world. His work is done today through his people. The church is a divine institution with a divine mission.

The work of the church is what Christians do collectively as an expression of their Christianity. It is what they do together "because they are Christians." The New Testament does not make a sharp distinction between individuals and the church. Letters are addressed to churches but talk about individual acts (1 Corinthians) or are addressed to individuals and talk about the assembly (1 Timothy and James). The church is the community of the saved, and in New Testament usage the church exists and one is a part of it whether it is assembled or not. The church is the corporate expression of Christianity; it is an inescapable part of being "in Christ." Worship may be done in private or in the assembly. Similarly the work of the church may be viewed as an individual activity or as the collective activity of the Lord's people.

The New Testament clearly envisages a service which is undertaken by the congregation as a whole, although it is necessarily carried out by particular members (Acts 6:1; 11:28–29; Rom. 15:25–27; 1 Cor. 16:1–4). It further describes a service which is a matter of individual responsibility and initiative, although it is also a contribution to the total service of the church (Rom. 12:20; Gal. 6:2). The individual should join the work undertaken by the congregation, but he is not thereby released from the obligation to minister on his own as a Christian individual; and the congregation cannot escape its responsibility on the pretext that ministering to the needs of others is the private responsibility of its members.

MINISTRY

Most of what has been written about the work of the church has been done from a practical standpoint. The purpose here is to look to the doctrinal grounding of the mission of the church. For this purpose, the work of the church may profitably be examined under the heading of ministry (*diakonia*). The word-group "minister" (deacon), "ministry" and "to minister" was used by the Greeks for menial, even servile activity. It could be used in a broad sense of general service rendered to another or in a narrow sense to serving at table or attending to bodily needs. The New Testament continues these non-specialized usages. But our interest is in the technical, doctrinal usages of the words. Here there is once more a broad meaning of Christ's service to people (Mk.10:45; Lk. 22:37) and of people's service to God (2 Cor. 6:4), to Christ (2 Cor. 11:23), to fellow disciples or the church as a whole (Mk. 9:35; Matt. 23:11; Col. 1:25). In the New Testament there is also a narrow technical use of the word-group, referring to the relief of the bodily and material needs of fellow Christians (Matt. 25:44; Rom. 15:25; Acts 6:2; 2 Cor. 8:19–20) and to the service of communicating the gospel (Acts 6:4; 2 Cor. 3:6; Col. 1:23, 1 Tim. 4:6). The analysis could be carried out extensively, for these words occur over one hundred times in the New Testament.

"Service" is, therefore, the comprehensive term for the "work" of the church. What is noteworthy is that the same terms describe Jesus' ministry and the Christian's ministry in the world.

Also notable is that a normally undignified word has been dignified with the highest calling in Christ Jesus. The work of the church is an act of obedience. The servant serves as he is commanded. He does not originate his actions. Neither does he need to justify his actions in service nor assume responsibility for the results. His Lord takes care of that. And there is no secondary motive for obedience; to obey is sufficient.

The kind of person Christ was and the kind of ministry he performed determine all Christian ministry. He took our human condition fully upon himself—all for a redemptive, re-creating purpose. As the church derives its nature from Jesus, even so the nature of the church's ministry is determined by that of her Lord.

It has been customary to classify the work of the church under three broad headings: evangelism, benevolence, and edification. These types of ministry are mutually interdependent, and the distinctions are somewhat artificial, but are useful in showing how the ministry of the church is rooted in Jesus.

EVANGELISM

Christ's personal ministry was characterized by preaching the gospel (Mk. 1:14–15; Lk. 4:18–19; Acts 10:36–37). Some reference to his preaching and teaching occurs in all the summaries of his earthly ministry. His directions to his disciples were to preach the gospel (Matt. 28:18–20; Lk. 24:46–49). The early church was found engaged in these activities (Acts 8:4).

The preaching work of the apostolic church is more than an example to be followed. Evangelism is the life blood of the church. This is the very reason for its existence—to convey the saving message of its Lord to a lost world. Calvary was incomplete without Pentecost. The revelation of the Christ-event must be communicated to people. The Great Commission was an act of the resurrected Christ. It is set in the heart of his redemptive acts— death, resurrection, ascension, and outpouring of the Holy Spirit. It appropriately comes at the close and climax of the Gospels. The preaching of the gospel provides the transition between the divine and the human sides of salvation. It establishes the fellowship in Christ. Preaching is God's planned way to unite his redemptive action in Christ and human appropriation of it. The man who makes a faithful exposition and application of God's message is bringing the Word of God to the people.

BENEVOLENCE

Jesus' ministry may be summarized as doing good to others (Matt. 4:23; 11:4–5; Acts 10:38). He fed the hungry, healed the sick, and released people from bondage to demons. Such acts were a demonstration that the Messianic Age was being inaugurated (Lk. 4:18–21). Jesus instructed his disciples similarly to care for those in need (Lk. 10:29–37; Matt. 25:31–46). The early church proved itself responsive to human needs (Rom. 12:13; 15:25–28; 2 Cor. 8–9; James 1:27). "Visitation" of the sick, imprisoned, and destitute in Biblical language did not mean a "social call," but a ministering to needs.

The New Testament church relieved human distress wherever it was found and the opportunity presented itself and not just within its own fellowship. The teachings of Jesus are clear (Matt. 5:43–48; 7:12; Lk. 10:25–37). The instructions to the churches also involve this same kind of love for all people (1 Thess. 3:12; 5:15; Rom. 12:9, 14, 20; Gal. 6:10). No restrictions are placed on the exercise of Christian charity by the church.

A love (Matt. 19:22) that stopped short of assisting one in need would be "in word" but not "in deed and truth" (1 John 3:18; cf. James 2:14–17). One could hardly pray "Give us this day our daily bread" (Matt. 6:11) and exclude others from the petition.

This assistance will include all human needs—such was the example of Jesus and such is involved in the teaching of Matthew 25:31–46. Human needs may include the necessities of life, illness, or mental and emotional problems. There seems no way to say that the church may clothe the naked but may not care for the sick, or to say that it may feed the hungry but may not nurture emotional maturity or counsel in marital problems.

Christians today lack the supernatural powers of Jesus to heal and cast out demons, but within their own gifts and resources they minister to the ill and resist the powers of evil.

EDIFICATION

Jesus spent much time instructing his disciples, as in Matthew 5–7. He often sought to be away from the crowds so that he could be alone with his disciples and teach them the mysteries of the kingdom for which the people were not ready. He directed these disciples not only to preach, but also to teach all he had taught them (Matt. 28:19–20). The apostolic church then was engaged in the task of Christian nurture, building up in the faith (Eph. 4:11–16; 2 Pet. 1:1–10; Gal. 6:6). This too is a broad category of concern, encompassing teaching, the whole sphere of Christian education, and developing disciples into the image of Christ.

SOME IMPLICATIONS

The church cannot be in Christ unless it is in him in all his ministering, in all his self-giving, in his meeting of human needs of all kinds, whether spiritual or physical. The church in Christ must carry on the messianic work. Its members are anointed and consecrated for service at their baptism, when they are incorporated into Christ and receive the Holy Spirit. This consecration of all members does not exclude a special authorization of certain members for certain tasks on behalf of the whole. But it does emphasize that all share Jesus' self consecration for humankind.

All phases of the work of the church—evangelism, benevolence, and edification—are a service or a ministry. When those who give or those who administer these services yield to the temptation of self-importance or lordliness, their work ceases to be a ministry as defined by the standard of Jesus. The church itself is needy and lives by the grace and gifts of God. It, therefore, cannot be patronizing toward those to whom it preaches or whom it helps. Whatever blessings the church bestows come not of itself. The church treats each person as a person, for it sees Christ in them (Matt. 25:35–45). When the church performs its work, there are to be no sounding trumpets (Matt. 6:2)—either before or after. If there seems to be a contradiction between Matthew 5:16 and 6:1, remember the tremendous difference between glorifying God and magnifying men.

These functions inhere in the nature of the church, as the church of Christ. Therefore, these functions, and the offices to perform them (evangelists, deacons, teachers), are permanent in the church (see further Lesson 12). These works of evangelism, benevolence, and edification have continued to characterize the ministry of the churches through the ages.

REVIEW QUESTIONS

1. How does the collective ministry of the church differ from the individual ministry of Christians?

2. How does the nature of the church (Lessons 3 and 4) determine the work of the church?

3. With the aid of a concordance elaborate on the different uses of the words ministry or service (*diakonia*), to serve (*diakonein*), and servant, minister or deacon (*diakonos*).

4. What are the traditional three main works of the church? Do you find this an adequate classification?

5. Establish the necessity for each main work from the practice of Jesus, the instructions he gave his disciples, and the example of the New Testament Church.

6. What activities were included within Jesus' benevolent work? What may legitimately be included within the church's service?

7. In what way are all Christians ministers?

8. What are some activities which may be included in the program of edification?

9. How must the church treat those to whom she ministers? Those to whom she preaches?

10. What is the proper expression of public relations in regard to the program of a church?

Lesson 11

MINISTRY IN THE CHURCH

"Joined and knit together by every joint with which it is supplied"
(Ephesians 4:16)

MINISTRY OF CHRIST

THE ESSENTIAL MINISTRY IN THE church is that of Jesus. He is called a "deacon," servant or minister (Rom. 15:8). He came to serve, or minister, and he offered that ministry as a pattern for his followers' ministry (Matt. 20:25–28). The truly essential work he performed was offering his "life as a ransom for many." This priestly ministry of atonement and mediation was performed once for all (Heb. 8:1–6; 9:11–14; 10:12–22; 1 Tim. 2:5–6). He still offers the eternal sacrifice and continues to intercede for his brethren, therefore there is no provision for a successor to Jesus' priestly ministry and no need for any functionaries to continue his priestly and sacrificial work.

Jesus Christ was God's greatest gift to his people. Among God's gifts to the church are the gifts of ministry or service. Specifically, these gifts are bestowed by the resurrected Christ (Eph. 4:7–11). When Christ's personal ministry on earth was completed, he entrusted the continuing aspects of his service into the hands of his disciples. The Gospels record how the resurrected Jesus, before his ascension to the right hand of the Father, commissioned the apostles to preach the gospel to the whole world (Matt. 28:18–20; Lk. 24:46–48). As equipment for this task he promised the guidance of the Holy Spirit (Lk. 24:49; Acts 1:8; John 20:22–23).

The Holy Spirit was to be "another Comforter," the "other self" of Jesus, empowering the continuation of Jesus' ministry in the world (John 14:16–17; 14:26). Other servants of the church were appointed as the church developed. They continue aspects of Jesus' ministry in the church.

There is need for ministers to convey the benefits of this priestly ministry to people and to continue the other aspects of Jesus' earthly ministry. He is the true Apostle (Heb. 3:1), Prophet (Acts 3:22–23), Teacher (John 1:38; 3:2; 13:13), Evangelist (Lk. 4:18), Pastor or Bishop (1 Pet. 2:25), and Deacon (Rom. 15:8). All ministry derives from Christ. Each of these named functionaries thus participates in the ministry of Christ and derives his function from Christ. In a partial way each continues some aspect of the whole service of God which flows from Christ to the church. Each finds the perfect pattern for his ministry in Jesus himself. Only in Christ do we learn what ministry really is.

MINISTRY OF BELIEVERS

Christ constitutes the standard for the exercise of ministry in the church. And he made plain in his teaching the path to greatness in the church (Matt. 20:20–28 and see below on the leadership of service). Authority (as exercised in the government, or the military, or in business, etc.) does not belong with the human leaders of the church. The words in the Greek language for official authority are noticeably absent from New Testament discussions of ministry. "Offices" in the church do not confer authority; they are functions or services to be performed (see further in the next lesson). They are a "work" (1 Tim. 3:1; 2 Tim. 4:5).

It is appropriate that the words "deacon" (*diakonos*, servant) and "ministry" (*diakonia*, service) should be used of everybody in the New Testament: Christ (Rom. 15:8), apostles (Matt. 20:26–28), evangelists (1 Tim. 4:6), Christians (John 12:26), civil magistrates (Rom. 13:4), waiters (John 2:5, 9), and an office in the church (Phil. 1:1). It is significant that the term for functions in the church which necessarily involve some measure of leadership has from the first been a word which signifies not preeminence or power but simply humble service and was the same word used of Christ's service to people and of the service owed by every Christian to God, to Christ, and to his fellows (Lesson 10).

GIFTS OF GRACE

Christ is not only the source and standard for ministry in the church, but he also gives the gifts which make this ministry possible. Before there is service, there are gifts, or qualifications, which the heavenly Lord has made available to all believers (1 Cor. 12:4–7, 28–31; Rom. 12:3–8; Eph. 4:7–8, 11–16; 1 Pet. 4:10–11). One notices from these passages that the offices or functions correspond to the talents or abilities of individuals. Moreover, what we may regard as natural abilities (note the list in Rom. 12:7–8), no less than supernatural endowments of the Spirit, are viewed as grace-gifts bestowed by the Lord on the church. Indeed the greatest gifts of the Spirit are open to all (1 Cor. 12:31–13:13; Gal. 5:22–23). Whatever a person has there is no cause for boasting and no basis for pride. "What have you that you did not receive? If then you received it, why do you boast as if it were not a gift?" (1 Cor. 4:7). The great variety of gifts considered in these passages is summed up by Peter under two headings—whoever speaks and whoever renders service (1 Pet. 4:11). There is a speaking ministry and a helping ministry, the ministry of the word and the ministry of tables (Acts 6:2–4), the ministry of teaching and the ministry of relief. Every function is a gift of grace.

USE OF GIFTS

God gives the ability, and with it he gives the opportunity and responsibility to use the gifts. This exercise is to be for the "common good" (1 Cor. 12:7), "for one another" (1 Pet. 4:10). Gifts are given not for selfish enjoyment but for the edification of the whole community. People must be "good stewards of God's varied grace" (1 Pet. 4:10). Whatever the gifts, they are to be used (Rom. 12:6).

Every Christian has some "gift." All in the church have the Holy Spirit (Acts 2:38; 5:32; 1 Cor. 6:19; Eph. 2:21). Thus spiritually all are equal and have the same rank. But this equality allows for the diversity of "gifts." The variety fits the dispositions and needs of all people. No one can feel that he is useless or not needed. However insignificant he may think his gift is, it is given by God and has a place in the upbuilding of the body and the carrying on of its activities (1 Cor. 12:14–26). Each one can develop that which he does best, and all contributing their part make for the unity and perfection of the whole (Eph. 4:12–16). This is a service, continuing the work of Jesus and inspired by the gifts he activates through his Spirit.

LEADERSHIP

Leadership is then based on the services rendered. Notice the following passages: "They have devoted themselves to the service of the saints; I urge you to be subject to such men" (1 Cor. 16:15–16); "Esteem them very highly in love because of their work" (1 Thess. 5:13); "Obey your leaders...for they are keeping watch over your souls" (Heb. 13:17). Submission is offered not because of some office held but because of the service performed. Such men who labor for the Lord naturally become leaders, and one gladly follows those who demonstrate their ability, their concern, and their service. Jesus, the Son of God, was an example in not arrogating authority to himself.

We see, therefore, that in the Scriptures the ideas of gift (qualification), service, and leadership are related. Out of these principles specific offices arise. Offices are based on the gifts possessed and the kind of service rendered. There is a formal recognition of the leadership exercised and earned.

APOSTLES AND PROPHETS

We may illustrate these principles now with a few words about some of the extraordinary functionaries of New Testament times. Then in the next lesson we will turn to those functionaries belonging to the continuing work of the church.

Christ first chose apostles to share in his ministry (Mk. 3: 14–15; Lk. 9:1–2; Matt. 28:16–20; John 20:21). The word apostle means "one sent," especially one sent with authority as the delegate of another. Jesus Christ was God's Apostle, the one sent by God (Heb. 3:1; John 13:20). The twelve were Jesus' apostles, the ones sent by him. "Apostle" was also used of messengers of the churches (2 Cor. 8:23) and of missionaries (Acts 14:4; 1 Cor. 9:5–6; Rom. 16:7). The background of the New Testament usage is probably to be found in the Jewish legal institution by which one could appoint an "apostle" who was as the sender himself and had full powers of attorney. "A man's *shaliach* (apostle) is like to himself," the Mishnah says.

The twelve were unique witnesses of the life and resurrection of Christ (Acts 1:16–22). Their qualifications gave them an unrepeatable office in the church. Jesus specially endowed them with the Holy Spirit for their work. There is thus a noticeable change in their status after the resurrection. They were most often called "disciples" during Jesus' personal ministry; the term "apostle" appears mainly in reference to the "limited commission" under which Jesus commissioned them to extend his ministry to the house of Israel (Matt. 10:1–23 and parallels). After the resurrection, they appear as apostles with the restrictions removed. They then acted authoritatively for Jesus. To deny apostolic authority is to deny the resurrection and to deny the commission of the Lord who sent them (see Lk. 10:16). The church rests on the apostolate (Eph. 2:20; Rev. 21:14), which required witness of the resurrection (Acts 1:21–22). As the witnesses of the resurrection of Christ (see Lesson 2 for the resurrection as constitutive of the church), the twelve became the foundation of the church. Not only did they call the church into existence by their preaching of the word, but they also gave authoritative instruction to the new converts and set in order the churches (Acts 6:1–6; 14:23).

The New Testament church also knew prophets (Eph. 2:20; 3:5) and other inspired men (1 Cor. 12:28). The exercise of their gifts spoke to the edification and encouragement of the church (1 Cor. 14:3). These were temporary functionaries: such was the realization of the post-New Testament church; such was implicit in the provisions made by the apostles in the later New Testament books for a settled ministry of men with natural qualifications; and such belongs to the nature of the case, for after the revelation was given and the church was established, the special guidance of inspired men was not needed.

The apostles and other inspired men, acting on behalf of Christ, established in the churches elders and deacons, and instructed evangelists and teachers to continue in the work of planting and upbuilding churches.

REVIEW QUESTIONS

1. Whose is the only essential ministry in the church? In what way?

2. How does all ministry in the church derive from Jesus?

3. What implications may be seen in the fact that the terms for each function in the church are applied to Jesus?

4. What is the path to greatness in the kingdom of God? How does this contrast with human standards?

5. Of what different persons is the word "deacon" (servant) used?

6. Summarize the teaching of 1 Corinthians 12:4–7, 28–31; Romans 12:3–8; Ephesians 4:7–16; 1 Peter 4:10–11 on ministry. What is the relationship of gifts and service?

7. Does the Christian have a place for pride in his attainments and abilities? How are his gifts to be exercised?

8. On what is leadership in the church based?

9. Discuss the meaning and New Testament usage of the word "apostle."

10. What is the permanent place of apostles in the church?

Lesson 12

OFFICES AND ORDINATION

"Set apart for the work"
(Acts 13:2)

ALL CHRISTIANS HAVE BEEN GIVEN A TASK, for service is rooted in the basic structure of one's existence in Christ (see Lessons 10 and 11). But certain ones are set apart by a commission to certain works.

Ministry, as we saw in the last lesson, is the gift of the resurrected Christ. Differing abilities and gifts come from God and are to be used for the common good (1 Cor. 12:7; 1 Pet. 4:10). Christ stands behind each ministry of service and is the perfect example of its exercise.

ORGANIZATION

The organization of the church inheres in the nature and work of the church. There are basic functions to be performed: There must be oversight and direction; there must be the preaching and teaching of the word; and there must be attention to human needs. The ministries of edification, evangelism, and benevolence constitute the basic ministries in the church. Thus the organization of the church is not arbitrary, but organic. It is involved in what is essential to the life of the church. There is organization about the church, but the church is not an organization. There is a given form in the New Testament which inheres in the nature of the church. As Titus 1:5 indicates, there is an established order in the church. This is not a "legalistic" form, but a functional arrangement. Within a basic pattern it allows all needed flexibility for performing the necessary mission of the church in the world.

Each church is the church—full and complete in itself. Each local church is the universal church in miniature. It is a manifestation of the whole. Thus Paul can address the "church of God which is at Corinth" (1 Cor. 1:2). This is the church of God as it has its manifestation at one place. The local church is not a "part" of the whole as if it were incomplete in itself and in need of more. Each local manifestation of the church is sufficient for its spiritual work. The church is always a visible body in the New Testament. The largest and only permanent visible organization of the church provided for in the New Testament is congregational. Thus no congregation or group of believers can exercise control over another (this is a prerogative which belongs to the Christ). Also, no one is "member at large"; he or she belongs to some local group of Christians.

ELDERS

The function of oversight is placed in the hands of men variously known as elders (presbyters), guardians (bishops), or shepherds (pastors). These words are used interchangeably with reference to the same group of men in each church in Acts 20:17, 28; 1 Peter 5:1–4; and Titus 1:5–7. The term "elders" derives from the Old Testament and the community organization of the Jews. This title suggests experience, spiritual maturity, and example of life. Elders would be the older respected men to whom others looked for leadership. The term "guardians" or "overseers" comes primarily from the Greek world, although Judaism knew functionaries similar in responsibility. The word had no special religious connotations and had to do with any kind of supervision or administration. It was a general word familiar to Greeks which could be taken over by Christians and given a religious significance in reference to those men with oversight of the church. "Shepherd" had a rich heritage in the ancient world;

it was already a figure for the kings and other leaders of God's people in the Old Testament (Ezek. 34:1–31). In the pastoral life with which nearly everyone was familiar in early times this word quickly called up the picture of the things a shepherd did for the care of his sheep.

The office of "elder" or "bishop" was a "work" or "place" (1 Tim. 3:1) in the church, evidently intended to be a permanent part of the church (Acts 14:23; Titus 1:5), for the work is a continuing necessity for the church and the apostles instructed the setting up of such men in the churches at a time when their personal supervision was to be withdrawn. Instructions about their qualifications may be learned from 1 Tim. 3 and Titus 1. Their work may be inferred from these qualifications and from the descriptive words entitling their office.

EVANGELISTS AND TEACHERS

In the letters to Timothy and Titus we find qualifications for "evangelists" (cf. 1 Tim. 4:12–16; 5:22; 2 Tim. 2:15–16, 24–26; 1 Tim. 6:3–11; 2 Tim. 4:1–5). These men are also termed "preacher" (Rom. 10:14), "minister" (1 Tim. 4:6—same word as "deacon"), "man of God" (1 Tim. 6:11). These men labored to win new converts either through traveling about or locating (Acts 8:40 and 21:8), strengthened the faith of those already converted (1 Tim. 4:6; Tit. 1:13; 2:1, 5), refuted error (1 Tim. 1:3), organized churches (Tit. 1:5), and engaged in the public ministry of the word (1 Tim. 4:13). Thus this was a specific function (2 Tim. 4:5) which inheres in the nature of the church, and therefore it was to be permanent (2 Tim. 2:2). The evangelists were servants of the Lord on behalf of people (cf. Col. 1:7).

Although the name "teachers" is not common in the New Testament (James 3:1), their work is everywhere. It belongs to the nature of Christianity as a teaching religion that there should always be need for such (Gal. 6:6).

DEACONS

Not a great deal is said about "deacons." The word itself refers to whoever renders service, of whatever kind, and thus is used in many different ways in the New Testament. As an office in the church it appears in close relationship with bishops (Phil. 1:1; 1 Tim. 3:8–13). Their qualifications in 1 Tim. 3 plus this association with bishops suggest that they are the assistants of the bishops and serve under their supervision in carrying out whatever phase of the work of the church may be assigned to them. The deacon in a particular way exemplifies the lowly service of Christ. According to the principle of Acts 6:2, deacons are naturally designed to handle the temporal and benevolent affairs of the church, but nothing restricts them to such. It may be doubted whether the seven in Acts 6 are deacons in the later sense, but we do have there the beginning of a differentiation of function in the church. There is a continuing need for servants who are trusted lieutenants of the eldership for carrying out the program of the church.

SELECTION AND INSTALLATION

Different methods of selection of functionaries in the church are reflected in the New Testament. There was choice by the Holy Spirit speaking through inspired prophets (Acts 13:1–3; 1 Tim. 1:18 and 4:14; cf. Acts 20:28). There was appointment by apostles and evangelists (Acts 14:23 probably indicates selection by Paul and Barnabas, or the whole process of appointment in which Paul and Barnabas took the lead). There was choice by the whole church (Acts 6:5; 2 Cor. 8:19; cf. Acts 15:22). In each case it should be noted that whoever took the initiative, the other members concurred. The other members of the church gave their recognition and endorsement. This was true even when there was a Spirit inspired selection: a human recognition of this choice followed (Acts 13:3; 1 Tim. 4:14).

The method of setting apart was uniform in the examples preserved. There was prayer accompanied by the laying on of hands in the appointment of evangelists (1 Tim. 4:14), missionaries (Acts 13:1–3), presumably elders (1 Tim. 5:22; Acts 14:23), and the seven (Acts 6:6). This installation may be performed by evangelists (Tit. 1:5; 1 Tim. 5:22), elders (1 Tim. 4:14), or apostles and prophets acting for the church (Acts 6:6; 13:3).

The laying on of hands is often understood as signifying the imparting of the Holy Spirit (Acts 8:15, 17). This was only one of the blessings, however, that might be bestowed in this way, and it is certainly inappropriate to the context of Acts 6:1–6 and 13:1–3 where it is already Spirit-filled men who received the laying on of hands. A gentle touching of the head of a person upon whom a blessing was pronounced was an Old Testament practice (Gen. 48:14). This particular gesture seems to have been a characteristic with Jesus (Mk. 5:23; 6:5; 8:23). The significance of placing the hand on another is well brought out in Mark 10:16—it was a way of bestowing a blessing. The accompanying benediction or prayer specified the type of blessing intended—perhaps a healing (Mk. 5:23), the imparting of the Holy Spirit (Acts 8:15, 17), or the appointment to a work in the church. Though the laying on of hands was thus a commonly accepted and well understood custom, it does not follow that one must receive this action in order to be a minister, but those who want to stay close to New Testament practices find no more appropriate way to appoint to office.

The significance of New Testament "ordination," or formal induction into office, is thus clear. It is the approval of the congregation which in this way gives its authorization to service; and it serves as the congregation's petition for divine favor upon those who undertake the specified ministry in the church. Acts 14:26 considered with 13:1–3 also shows this. In sum, "ordination" is a formal "setting apart," in which one is dedicated to a work and commended to God in its performance. Though the "how" is not specified in detail it should be dignified and orderly.

Acts 6:1–6 gives the fullest picture in an orderly sequence of the New Testament practice of appointing to office, and it may be taken as typical of the principles we have set forth. There was a teaching on the need and the qualifications of the men to fill the need (Acts 6:2–3); a "looking out" by the congregation (Acts 6:3—the method of "examining" is not given but the men chosen were "tested" men); a choice (Acts 6:5—again the method is not given but the choice constituted a recognition by the congregation that these men possessed the required qualities); a presentation (Acts 6:6—this was an endorsement and authorization by the congregation, a formal recognition); and after being presented for approval of the spiritual leaders, a prayer and the laying on of hands (Acts 6:6—the benediction of the church and its petition to God). In sum we note that the whole congregation was involved; the procedure was orderly; it was formal and in the presence of all; and both leaders and people knew one another and their mutual responsibilities.[7]

DOCTRINAL MEANING

These procedures are part of a doctrinal context. The important truth being conveyed is that God chooses ministers for his church. Whoever the human instruments of this choice, ministers are God's gifts to his people. The word for "ordination" (*cheirotonia*) was commonly used in Hellenistic Jewish writers for all of God's appointments. In the church God institutes the office, sets the qualifications, and makes possible the attainment of the office. We have Spirit appointed bishops (Acts 20:28) today when we have men with the qualifications set by the Spirit. Even so, there must be the concurrence of those whom they lead just as there was the human recognition in New Testament times. This realization should bring home the importance and seriousness of being the organ of divine choice. It is our responsibility to choose the man God would choose.

7   Everett Ferguson, "Ordination in the Early Church IV: Ordination in the First Century," *The Early Church at Work and Worship*, Volume 1 (Eugene: Cascade, 2013), 92–110.

Furthermore, whom God ordains, he blesses. Thus the ordination is set in a context of prayer. The blessing of the congregation finds its counterpart in God's equipment and blessing upon the man for his work.

Finally, the church ordains particular individuals for the work which is the work of the whole church. It does so not because they are to do for others something which is not their responsibility. Nor can one pay someone to discharge his work for the Lord. Rather the church appoints them because they objectify to the church its own ministry within the world. It supports them in this work because they are an embodiment and representation of what the whole church is. Ministry represents to the church the nature of its own vocation. Ministers (elders, deacons, etc.) personify the work of the whole church, and the church's ministry is Christ's ministry.

LATER DEVELOPMENTS

The churches in the New Testament for which we have information were led by a plurality of elders (also called bishops or pastors) assisted by deacons. The earliest departure from New Testament practice as far as our documentation goes was in the organization of local churches. Already in the early second century some churches had one bishop (as chief elder) at the head of the college of presbyters (elders).[8] A hierarchy of bishops developed in time with the bishop of the principal church of a province being designated a metropolitan bishop, and he presided at councils of clergy in his province. The centralizing of authority climaxed with the recognizing of five patriarchs (the bishops of Rome, Constantinople, Alexandria, Antioch, and Jerusalem). The bishop of Rome became the Pope over the Latin-speaking churches of western Europe. Along with the hierarchical development was the limiting of priestly language and duties to the bishop by the third century and then to the presbyters.

---

8   Everett Ferguson, *Early Christians Speak*, 3rd edition (Abilene: ACU Press, 1999), 163-175.

REVIEW QUESTIONS

1. How does the New Testament presentation of local churches support the concept of "congregational autonomy"?

2. Relate the offices of elder, evangelist, and deacon to the threefold work of the church.

3. What passages suggest that the terms "elder," "bishop," and "pastor" are interchangeable in the New Testament? How is this shown by these passages?

4. From these descriptive words and from their qualifications what can be inferred about the work of these men?

5. How may it be shown that functions of each office—elder, evangelist, and deacon—belongs to the permanent structure of the church?

6. What different methods of selection for work in the church are found in the New Testament?

7. What methods of installation into office may be found in the New Testament?

8. What is the meaning of the gesture of "laying on hands"?

9. Describe the procedure of selecting and setting apart the seven in Acts 6.

10. What doctrinal lessons may we learn from the teaching about ordination in the New Testament? What practical consequences will this have?

Lesson 13

THE KINGDOM AND THE CHURCH

"Made us a kingdom"
(Revelation 1:6)

MEANING OF "KINGDOM"

THE UNDERLYING MEANING OF THE Hebrew and Greek words translated kingdom is kingship, royal power, royal rule. Kingdom in the Bible primarily refers to reign and not realm (Rev. 11:15). An examination of the passages (e.g. Dan. 4:31, 36) will show this meaning. Kingdom is thus an active, not a static word, and the kingdom of God is something God does and not something humans achieve. But of course God's rule does not operate in a void. It implies a people living under that rule; hence sometimes the word kingdom has the derivative meaning of realm.

When one realizes that kingdom refers to God's kingly authority, then it is evident that God always has a kingdom, although there have been different manifestations of it. The kingdom was a present reality in the faith of the Old Testament (Ex. 15:18; 1 Sam. 12:12; Ps. 103:19; 145:11–13). But while God was always king, there was also the expectation of a future manifestation of God's sovereignty when he would exercise kingship in a fuller way over the nations (Isa. 24:23; 33:22; Zeph. 3:15; Zech. 14:16–17).

When Jesus came preaching, "The time is fulfilled," "The kingdom is at hand" (Matt. 4:17, 23; Mk. 1:14–15; Lk. 4:43), the people recognized that the Old Testament hope was being realized and God was beginning to manifest his kingship in a new way. The word translated "at hand" expresses the idea of "breaking in." Thus Jesus most often can present the kingdom as yet future (Matt. 6:10; Mk. 9:1; Matt. 25:34; Lk. 13:29), but in a few passages he speaks of the power of the kingdom as a present reality in his own ministry (Lk. 11:20; 17:21). His miracles were a sign of the Messianic Age. God's kingly power was at work through Jesus.

The same dual aspect of present and future may be observed in the New Testament epistles. Christians are already in a kingdom (Col. 1:13), but they look for entrance into the kingdom in the future (2 Tim. 4:18). In this perspective one may examine the relationship between church and kingdom. There are some passages where the terms appear interchangeable (Matt. 16:18–19; Heb. 12:23, 28; Rev. 1:4, 6, 9). But from the other passages given above it is clear that church and kingdom are not simply correlative terms so that wherever one sees the word kingdom he is to understand the church. They do, however, have a point of overlap. The kingdom creates a community; those who accept the rule of God constitute the church.

Christians have the advantage of living further along in God's history of salvation. The Messianic Age has been inaugurated. There has been a further manifestation of God's kingdom. With the coming of Jesus and his death, resurrection, and outpouring of the Holy Spirit there is a new stage in history. The Messianic Age (Joel 2:28–32) is realized in the person of Jesus (Acts 2:36). Acceptance of him is acceptance of the kingdom. There has been an overthrow of the powers which rule this world of darkness (Lk. 10:17–20; Col. 2:15). But their influence has not been abolished (Eph. 6:10–17). We still live in this "present evil age" (Gal. 1:4). But the "powers of the age to come" (Heb. 6:5) have already invaded this world and become available to people in Christ. The final victory is certain and will be consummated at the second coming (1 Cor. 15:24–28). At Pentecost the lordship of Jesus was proclaimed and the church was gathered of those receiving the promises of God and living for the future.

SOME IMPLICATIONS

From this standpoint of "inaugurated eschatology" (last events begun) a number of New Testament passages take on fresh meaning. The Christian age is the "last days" (Acts 2:16–17; Heb. 1:2). This is the last dispensation or period of time, for the events of the end time have been inaugurated. The gift of the Spirit is a "guarantee" (Eph. 1:14; 2 Cor. 1:22), the "first fruits" (Rom. 8:23), a first installment of the blessings of the world to come (Rom. 8:11) when there will be a fulfillment of what has begun now. In this light, one can understand how eternal life may be spoken of as a present possession (1 John 5:11, 13; John 5:24) as well as a future hope (Rom. 6:22; John 12:25). The quality of life that belongs to the world to come is now the Christian's. He may indeed fall away from it, but if he does not have that life now, he will never obtain it. The "new creation" has begun in Christ (2 Cor. 5:17).

There is thus a tension set up for the Christian between the "now" and the "not yet." He has a foretaste but not a fulfillment of God's blessings. The Christian has a different world view, for he looks beyond this world to the world to come. But he still lives in this world, yet he does so by the standards and power of the world to come.

Among the implications which this information has for the understanding of the New Testament, mention may be made of the petition in the Lord's prayer, "Thy kingdom come" (Matt. 6:10). Realizing that God's kingdom is a much broader concept than realm or territory makes this petition always appropriate. Moreover, the structure of the clauses suggests more about this petition. The three petitions, "Hallowed be thy name," "Thy kingdom come," and "Thy will be done," are all qualified by the phrase, "On earth as it is in heaven." The prayer asks that God's kingdom come and God's name be hallowed, no less than God's will be done, on earth as it is in heaven. God's kingship is supreme in heaven; the disciple prays for the fulfillment on earth.

SUMMARY

By relating the church to the kingdom, it becomes evident that the church is the eschatological community, the people created by the kingdom, the people living in the "now and the not yet," the people of the end time who have a special purpose in God's plans. The perspectives gained from a consideration of the kingdom may be used in summarizing the lessons of this series.

Christ as the king (Rev. 17:14) and the power of God (1 Cor. 1:24) brings the kingdom in his person, so wherever he is, there is the kingdom in person (Matt. 12:28). The kingdom is exclusively God's business; it cannot, be built by human beings. But the kingly activity of God establishes a community as he calls people to obedience. Thus instead of Jesus restoring the kingdom to Israel (Acts 1:6) his kingdom established a new Israel. The lordship or kingship of Jesus is confessed and expressed in one's baptism. The rule of God comes to people when Jesus forgives sins (Matt. 18:21–23). Jesus gives a new life, and he manifests his divine power in forgiveness (Mk. 2:1–12). The power of Satan is broken (Lk. 10:1–20), and this continues to occur when his heralds proclaim the kingdom. Salvation delivers one from subjection to "the world rulers of this present darkness" (Eph. 6:12). Their power is broken and will finally be destroyed (2 Tim. 1:10; 1 Cor. 15:26). The Christian is no longer subject (to law, death, Devil, sin) but is free in Christ Jesus (Rom. 6–7; Gal. 4; 1 Cor. 15:51–57; Col. 2:14–15). One who is "in Christ" rules with Christ, for he shares in his kingdom (Rev. 5:9–10) and "shall reign with him" (2 Tim. 2:12). The church in its work continues the kingly ministry of Jesus as it proclaims the word of power, the message of deliverance (Rom. 1:16; Eph. 3:7).

Christian ethics are "kingdom ethics," not ethics for those outside the church. They are given to those who come under God's rule, and indeed are meaningful only to those who seek to do God's will. The kingdom is an ethical as well as an eschatological category in the New Testament (Rom. 14:17). The Christian tries to translate the standards of another plane of existence into the present human situation.

The fellowship established in Christ with one another continues. The events of the end time do not break this fellowship (1 Thess. 4:17; 1 John 3:2). Eschatology is "to be with Christ" (Phil. 1:21–23). Present fellowship in Christ gives hope (Rom. 8:24–25; 1 Thess. 4:13). The coming of the Lord will be a time of "gathering together" (Matt. 24:31; 2 Thess. 2:1). The church as the community of the saved is found in assembly now (Heb. 10:25). Its present gathering together anticipates the final assembly in the presence of the Lord. The church assembled in worship is an anticipation of the coming of Christ. Worship is thus an eschatological act; it is oriented toward the end time. In worship the church gathered around Christ is engaged in a foretaste of the heavenly worship (Rev. 4–5). Particularly in the Lord's supper does the church share the meal of the world to come (Matt 26:29; Lk. 22:16, 18).

The church must continue the king's work. No earthly failure need discourage the church, since the greatest earthly failure is at the center of its faith—the cross. But it was by this very cross that Jesus triumphed over the forces of evil, to be exalted as Lord at God's right hand (1 Pet. 3:21–22). The church thus enjoys the steadfastness of hope (1 Thess. 1:3).

The coming of the Lord is a matter of joyful anticipation for the church and an event for which it prays (1 Cor. 16:22; Rev. 22:20). There is not fear, for the church already partakes of the character of that coming (1 Thess. 5:4–11). It is the community of the last days, it belongs to that Day. Therefore, the end time will be in continuity with the church's present experience with the Lord. Then God's kingdom will be complete (1 Cor. 15:24–28; Rev. 21:5–22:5).

In the New Testament the kingdom (the rule) of God is both present and future. In the second century the kingdom was viewed by orthodox writers almost exclusively as future,[9] and this usage of kingdom as primarily a heavenly reality has continued to the present. Hence, the present reality of the kingship of God is often overlooked and its importance neglected. That kingship is meant to be implemented and experienced in the church.

REVIEW QUESTIONS

1. Define the Hebrew and Greek words translated kingdom.

2. Consult a concordance for passages in the Old Testament and New Testament using the word kingdom. With the aid of a good Bible dictionary or encyclopedia prepare a classification of the usages of the word kingdom.

3. In what way is God's kingdom always both present and future for human beings?

4. How do the events of Acts 2 mark a further stage in the progress of God's kingdom among men? How are these events anticipated in the ministry of Jesus?

5. The term "inaugurated eschatology" has been used to describe the New Testament perspective. Do you find this adequate?

---

9   Everett Ferguson, "The Kingdom of God in Early Patristic Literature," in *The Early Church at Work and Worship*, volume 2 (Eugene: Cascade, 2014), 176-199.

6. How does this perspective relate to such ideas as the gift of the Spirit, eternal life, new creation, and other New Testament terms?

7. May a Christian still pray the Lord's prayer now that the church has come? On what basis do you give your answer?

8. Is there any evidence that there will be a special reign of Christ on earth after his second coming?

9. Relate the idea of the church as the eschatological community to preceding lessons in this series.

10. What relationship do Christians sustain to the world to come? What then should be their attitude toward the Lord's coming?

Selected Bibliography

Banks, Robert. *Paul's Idea of Community*. Grand Rapids: Eerdmans, 1980.

Basden, Paul, and David S. Dockery, eds. T*he People of God: Essays on the Believer's Church*. Nashville: Broadman, 1991.

Bouyer, Louis. *The Church of God, Body of Christ, and Temple of the Spirit*. Chicago: Franciscan, 1982.

Bright, John. *The Kingdom of God*. Nashville: Abingdon, 1953.

Bromiley, G. W. *Christian Ministry*. Grand Rapids: Eerdmans, 1960.

Campbell, Alexander. *The Christian System*. Cincinnati: Standard, reprint.

Ferguson, Everett. *The Church of Christ: A Biblical Ecclesiology for Today*. Grand Rapids: Eerdmans, 1996.

Flew, R. N. *Jesus and His Church*. London: Epworth, 1943.

Giles, Kevin. *What on Earth Is the Church? An Exploration in New Testament Theology*. Downers Grove: InterVarsity, 1995.

Hays, Richard. *The Moral Vision of the New Testament*. San Francisco: Harper Collins, 1996.

Lohfink, Gerhard. *Jesus and Community*. London: SPCK, 1985.

Kruse, Colin. *New Testament Models of Ministry: Jesus and Paul*. Nashville: Thomas Nelson, 1983.

Kung, Hans. *The Church*. New York: Sheed and Ward, 1967.

Martin, Ralph. *Worship in the Early Church*. Westwood: Revell, 1964.

Milligan, Robert. *The Scheme of Redemption*. St. Louis: Bethany, reprint.

Minear, Paul, *Images of the Church in the New Testament*. Philadelphia: Westminster, 1960.

Restoration Quarterly. Vol. 2, No.4 (1958). Abilene.

Schnackenburg, Rudolf. *The Church in the New Testament*. New York: Herder and Herder, 1965.

Schweizer, Eduard. *The Church as the Body of Christ*. Richmond: John Knox, 1964.

Watson, David. *I Believe in the Church*. Grand Rapids: Eerdmans, 1978.

Willis, Wendell. *When You Come Together: The Theology and Practice of Congregational Worship*. Austin: Christian Studies Press, 2010.

INDEX OF BIBLICAL PASSAGES

118

119

122

126

INDEX OF SUBJECTS

Pentecost 18-19, 21, 42, 83, 108.

people 11, 20, 23, 42, 50, 53-54, 57-59, 82-85, 90-92, 107, 110; of God 12, 14-15, 16, 20-21, 25-30, 33-34, 37, 41-44, 47, 49, 51-52, 55, 67, 69-70, 73, 75-77, 81-82, 89, 99, 102, 107-108, 110.

Peter 14, 17-21, 23, 51, 91.

power 19-21, 27, 41-44, 46-47, 53-54, 63, 77, 85, 90-91, 93, 107-110.

praise 69, 77.

pray 22, 67, 69-70, 74, 84, 101-103, 109, 111, 113.

preach 19-22, 36, 42, 47 50, 60, 68-70, 83-85, 87, 89, 93, 97, 99, 107.

presbyter 98, 103.

priest 11-12, 17, 25, 27, 30, 89-90, 103.

promise 17-18, 20-21, 42, 44-45, 47, 69, 89, 108.

prophet 11-12, 15, 44, 47, 75, 90, 93-94, 100-101.

Qumran community 12.

redeem 11-13, 50-51, 54, 66, 73, 83-84, 77.

repent 13, 20, 41, 45-47.

resurrection 17-22, 27, 41-43, 47, 73, 77-78, 83, 89, 93, 97, 108.

righteous 14, 25.

rock 17-18, 22. see also stone

sacrifice 44, 60, 67, 69, 75-79, 89.

saint(s) 26-29, 31, 57, 60, 92.

salvation 20, 26, 35, 41-43, 47, 54, 59, 67, 74, 81, 84, 108, 110-111.

servant 11-12, 18, 26, 51, 57, 83, 86, 89-90, 95, 99-100.

service 53, 59, 65, 68, 70, 81-83, 85-87, 89-92, 95, 97, 100, 101.

shepherd 98-99.

sign 11, 19-20, 43, 60, 108.

sin 13-16, 20-21, 41, 43-44, 46, 48-51, 61, 69, 75, 78, 110.

Sinai 13, 25.

sing 67, 69-70.

song 67, 69-70.

stone 18, 22, 37. see also rock

submit 36, 38, 62, 92.

suffer 17-19.

ABOUT THE AUTHOR

Everett Ferguson earned B.A. and M.A. degrees from Abilene Christian University and S.T.B. and Ph.D. degrees from Harvard University. He taught Bible, Greek, and Church History at Abilene Christian University from 1962 to 1998. He holds membership in the Society of Biblical Literature, the American Society of Church History (member of the council, 1983-85), North American Patristics Society (president, 1990-92), Association internationale d'études patristiques (member of the council 1995-2003), and Conference on Faith and History.

Ferguson's awards include honorary John Harvard Fellow at Harvard, twice teacher of the year in his division at Abilene Christian, John G. Gammie Senior Lecturer of the Southwest Commission for Religious Studies (1996-97), a Festschrift, *The Early Church in Its Context: Essays in Honor of Everett Ferguson* (Leiden: Brill, 1998), plaques for Christian service from numerous institutions and organizations, and *Eucharist and Ecclesiology* for his eightieth birthday (Eugene: Cascade, forthcoming).

A prolific author, Ferguson has published major books: *The Church of Christ: A Biblical Ecclesiology for Today* (Grand Rapids: Eerdmans, 1996), translated into Korean and Russian; *Backgrounds of Early Christianity* (third edition; Grand Rapids: Eerdmans, 2003), translated into Korean and Chinese; *Early Christians Speak*, 2 volumes (Abilene: ACU Press, 1999, 2002— translated into Russian); *Church History*, Volume 1: *From Christ to Pre-Reformation* (second edition; Grand Rapids: Zondervan,

2013; accompanying video lectures 2016); *Baptism in the Early Church: History, Theology, and Liturgy in the First Five Centuries* (Grand Rapids: Eerdmans, 2009); and *Understandings of the Church* (Minneapolis: Fortress, forthcoming). Collected articles and shorter books include: *The Early Church and Today*, 2 volumes (Abilene: ACU Press, 2012, 2014); *The Early Church at Work and Worship*, 3 volumes (Eugene: Cascade, 2013--); *Collected Popular Articles and Lectures* (Walton: Yeomen Press, 2013); *The Rule of Faith: A Guide* (Eugene: Cascade, 2015); *A Cappella Music in the Public Worship of the Church* (fourth edition; Abilene: Desert Willow, 2013; an earlier edition translated into Spanish); *Women in the Church: Biblical and Historical Perspectives* (second edition; Abilene: Desert Willow, 2015; first edition translated into German). His extensive editorial work includes the *Encyclopedia of Early Christianity* (second edition; New York: Garland [Taylor and Francis], 1997).

Ferguson served for nineteen years as an elder of the Hillcrest Church of Christ in Abilene, TX. He has preached, lectured, and taught in many parts of the U. S. and many other countries. He and Nancy, his wife of sixty years, have three children, six grandchildren, and one great grandchild.